Bond
No.1 for exam success

Verbal Reasoning

Assessment Papers

Up to Speed

10–11+ years

OXFORD
UNIVERSITY PRESS

Great Clarendon Street, Oxford, OX2 6DP, United Kingdom

Oxford University Press is a department of the University of Oxford.
It furthers the University's objective of excellence in research,
scholarship, and education by publishing worldwide. Oxford is
a registered trade mark of Oxford University Press in the UK and in
certain other countries

Text © Frances Down 2015

The moral rights of the authors have been asserted

First published in 2015
This edition published in 2022

All rights reserved. No part of this publication may be reproduced,
stored in a retrieval system, or transmitted, in any form or by any
means, without the prior permission in writing of Oxford University
Press, or as expressly permitted by law, by licence or under terms
agreed with the appropriate reprographics rights organization.
Enquiries concerning reproduction outside the scope of the above
should be sent to the Rights Department, Oxford University Press, at
the address above.

You must not circulate this work in any other form and you must
impose this same condition on any acquirer

British Library Cataloguing in Publication Data
Data available

978-0-19-278515-2

10 9 8 7 6 5 4 3 2 1

Paper used in the production of this book is a natural, recyclable
product made from wood grown in sustainable forests.
The manufacturing process conforms to the environmental
regulations of the country of origin.

Printed in Great Britain by Ashford Colour Press Ltd.

Acknowledgements

The publishers would like to thank the following for permissions to
use copyright material:

Page make-up: OKS Prepress, India
Cover illustrations: Lo Cole

Although we have made every effort to trace and contact all
copyright holders before publication this has not been possible in all
cases. If notified, the publisher will rectify any errors or omissions at
the earliest opportunity.

Links to third party websites are provided by Oxford in good faith
and for information only. Oxford disclaims any responsibility for
the materials contained in any third party website referenced in
this work.

Introduction

What is Bond?

The Bond *Up to Speed* titles are part of the Bond range of assessment papers, the number one series for the 11+, selective exams and general practice. Bond *Up to Speed* is carefully designed to support children who need less challenging activities than those in the regular age-appropriate Bond papers, in order to build up and improve their techniques and confidence.

How does this book work?

The book contains two distinct sets of papers, along with full answers and a Progress Chart.

- Focus tests, accompanied by advice and directions, are focused on particular (and age-appropriate) verbal reasoning question types encountered in the 11+ and other exams. The questions are deliberately set at a less challenging level than the standard *Assessment Papers*. Each Focus test is designed to help a child 'catch' their level in a particular question type, and then gently raise it through the course of the test and the subsequent Mixed papers.

- Mixed papers are longer tests containing a full range of verbal reasoning question types. These are designed to provide rigorous practice with less challenging questions, perhaps against the clock, in order to help children acquire and develop the necessary skills and techniques for 11+ success.

Full answers are provided for both types of test in the middle of the book.

How much time should the tests take?

The tests are for practice and to reinforce learning, and you may wish to test exam techniques and working to a set time limit. Using the Mixed papers, we would recommend that your child spends 50 minutes answering the 75 questions in each paper.

You can reduce the suggested time by 5 minutes to practise working at speed.

Using the Progress Chart

The Progress Chart can be used to track Focus test and Mixed paper results over time to monitor how well your child is doing and identify any repeated problems in tackling the different question types.

Focus test 1 — Words that are similar

> Always read this type of question carefully, as most of them will have similar *and* opposite options.

Find a word that is similar in meaning to the word in capital letters and that rhymes with the second word.

Example CABLE tyre <u>WIRE</u>

> If you cannot find a suitable similar word, try experimenting with rhyming words.

1 MARSH   dog   _____
2 BAND   dealt   _____
3 DEPART   grieve _____
4 DISCOVER wind   _____
5 HINT   dew   _____
6 LIFT   days   _____

Underline the two words, one from each group, that are the closest in meaning.

Example (race, shop, <u>start</u>)   (finish, <u>begin</u>, end)

> Take one word from the left brackets and match it against the words in the right brackets. Repeat until you find the <u>most</u> similar pair.

7 (roam, rush, hurry)   (break, ponder, wander)
8 (harbour, sea, cliff)   (waves, port, ferry)
9 (slop, slip, slap)   (slope, slide, stamp)
10 (colourful, sensitive, pathetic) (pitiable, wonderful, joyous)
11 (near, neat, untidy)   (far, patchy, tidy)
12 (lie, truth, fib)   (recover, recline, reckon)

Underline the pair of words most similar in meaning.

Example come, go   <u>roams, wanders</u>   fear, fare

13. war, peace   calm, serene   quiet, noise
14. warm, tepid   boiling, freezing   hot, cold
15. slim, plump   bulk, mass   height, weight
16. storm, fine   cloud, rain   wind, meander
17. hurry, rush   hour, minute   trip, trap
18. cow, bull   chilly, warm   swelling, lump

More than one pair may have similar meanings. Look for the most appropriate.

Underline the word in the brackets that goes best with the words given outside the brackets.

Example word, paragraph, sentence   (pen, cap, <u>letter</u>, top, stop)

19. portion, ration, share   (meal, eat, aiding, part, full)
20. Friday, Saturday, Sunday   (May, date, Wednesday, winter, weekend)
21. Severn, Trent, Mersey   (Nile, Amazon, Rhone, Thames, Tiber)
22. peril, danger, threat   (hazard, safety, chance, death, worry)
23. mother, father, brother   (grandfather, aunt, niece, grandson, sister)
24. puff, blow, gasp   (breathe, pant, sigh, moan, inhale)

Look at the pair of words on the left. Underline the one word in the brackets that goes with the word outside the brackets in the same way as the first two words go together.

Make sure you match the second pair of words in the same way as the first.

Example good, better   bad, (naughty, worst, <u>worse</u>, nasty)

25. howl, wail   whisper, (shout, murmur, cry, talk)
26. higher, advanced   lower, (basic, underground, inside, deeper)
27. bright, shiny   cheerful, (chatty, negative, positive, gloomy)
28. ripe, mature   foolish, (wet, silly, childish, messy)
29. internal, inside   external, (eternal, exterior, outlook, extra)
30. blind, bind   flame, (fire, lame, fame, foam)

Now go to the Progress Chart to record your score!   Total   30

Focus test 2 — Words that are opposite

Find a word that is opposite in meaning to the word in capital letters and that rhymes with the second word.

Example SHARP   front   <u>BLUNT</u>

1. DULL   tiny   _____
2. LIGHT   park   _____
3. POOR   ditch   _____
4. DIFFICULT dimple   _____
5. SMOOTH   cuff   _____
6. WHISPER   doubt   _____

If you cannot find a suitable opposite word, try experimenting with rhyming words.

Underline the two words, one from each group, that are opposite in meaning.

Example (dawn, <u>early</u>, wake)   (<u>late</u>, stop, sunrise)

7. (hold, nudge, bond)   (release, rescue, clasp)
8. (lazy, busy, brisk)   (breezy, idle, hurry)
9. (open, closed, ajar)   (door, slam, shut)
10. (murky, scary, timid)   (frightened, bold, shy)
11. (asleep, daytime, doze)   (snore, dreaming, awake)
12. (short, slim, slow)   (sluggish, quick, brief)

Underline the pair of words most opposite in meaning.

Example cup, mug   coffee, milk   <u>hot, cold</u>

13. pity, regret   high, low   black, dark
14. plus, minus   probable, likely   pound, hit
15. scowl, scone   plan, scheme   grand, humble
16. bite, chew   intend, mean   strong, weak
17. work, play   cling, adhere   sport, games
18. please, satisfy   best, worst   wander, wonder

Underline the word in the brackets that is most opposite in meaning to the word in capitals.

Example WIDE (broad vague long <u>narrow</u> motorway)

> Pick the <u>most</u> opposite. Work through, word by word.

19 WORTHLESS (wandering valuable wealthy poor hopeless)
20 LIVELY (lethargic energetic bouncy quite bubbly)
21 FLOAT (glide drift sink swim dive)
22 SERIOUS (sensible foolish dangerous intent keen)
23 PECULIAR (normal odd splendid strange morose)
24 TENDER (painful bruised raw loving tough)

Underline the two words that are the odd ones out in the following group of words.

Example black <u>king</u> purple green <u>house</u>

> Three of the words have something in common. Look for the link. In the example, it is colours.

25 coarse fine wet delicate dainty
26 cheetah leopard wolf lion fox
27 entire part complete portion whole
28 silly idiotic stupid brave unjust
29 mortar pebble cement stone rock
30 disturb peace agitate worry calm

Now go to the Progress Chart to record your score!   Total 30

Focus test 3 — Sorting words

Look at these groups of words.

A	B	C	D
Breeds of dog	Colours	Footwear	Body parts

Choose the correct group for each of the words below. Write in the letter.

1. blue ____   terrier ____   boxer ____
2. sandal ____   arm ____   boot ____
3. red ____   slipper ____   shoe ____
4. chest ____   head ____   green ____

Rearrange the muddled words in capital letters in the following sentences so that they make sense.

Example There are sixty SNODCES <u>seconds</u> in a UTMINE <u>minute</u>.

> Use the sense of the sentence to help you. Be careful with spelling.

5. Noon, or DDAMIY _____, is the same as VELTWE _____ o'clock.

6. Last NDSUAY _____ we saw the new film at the NMECIA _____.

7. We heaped our LAPSET _____ when we were offered NDOESC _____ helpings.

8. PRISGN _____ is the SSNOEA _____ of the year when the flowers begin to blossom.

9. Dad HVSADE _____ off his DREAB _____ over the weekend.

10. Mum was upset when our TTNEKI _____ climbed the bedroom CTRUANIS _____.

Rearrange the letters in capitals to make another word. The new word has something to do with the first two words or phrases.

Example spot   soil   SAINT   <u>STAIN</u>

First look at the clues, then rearrange the letters to find the anagram.

11 extra   unused   SPEAR   _____
12 ledge   sill   FLESH   _____
13 grin   beam   LIMES   _____
14 bargain   cut-price PEACH   _____
15 gaze   watch   RATES   _____
16 fraud   swindler   TEACH   _____

Underline the two words that are made from the same letters.

Example TAP   PET   <u>TEA</u>   POT   <u>EAT</u>

Scan the words quickly and see if a pair jumps out. If you don't see the answer, look through, word by word, at individual letters.

17 LEAST   CLONE   STOLE   TALES   STONE
18 CLAIM   ANGEL   GLEAN   GRIME   MERGE
19 BROTH   THOSE   SHORT   THROB   BEAST
20 THUMB   BRUNT   THORN   TENOR   NORTH
21 STONE   ATONE   TOAST   STEAL   NOTES
22 NESTS   SNARE   NEARS   SNORE   STORE

Underline the one word in each group that **cannot be made** from the letters of the word in capital letters.

Example STATIONERY   stone   tyres   ration   <u>nation</u>   noisy

Look for any letters that are not in the word in capitals, and for repeats of letters.

23 BLEEDING   blend   glide   blind   bling   globe
24 SPRAINED   drips   nears   spear   drain   stain

| 25 | APOLOGIES | pools | gloss | goals | gapes | loops |
| 26 | SHAMEFUL | flash | fuels | flame | marsh | flush |

Underline the one word in each group that **can be made** from the letters of the word in capital letters.

| Example | CHAMPION | camping | notch | peach | cramp | <u>chimp</u> |

Take care with vowels particularly.

27	POURED	droop	rowdy	prowl	pours	proud
28	HEXAGONS	enough	shown	ashen	ghost	agent
29	CONSTANT	taint	scant	scone	stone	state
30	BROUGHT	cough	budge	throb	bright	taught

Focus test 4 — Selecting words

Complete the following sentences by selecting the most sensible word from each group of words given in the brackets. Underline the words selected.

Example The (<u>children</u>, boxes, foxes) carried the (houses, <u>books</u>, steps) home from the (greengrocer, <u>library</u>, factory).

> Read the sentence carefully first and try to spot the most likely words that will make the sentence make sense. Then work through each sentence, bracket by bracket, choosing the most appropriate word from each one.

1. We (bought, carried, threw) our air (tickets, whistles, balloons) yesterday to go to (Spain, the zoo, the picnic).

2. On the underground (car, train, aeroplane), we had to travel eight (stops, starts, hints) before we reached the (bridge, station, end) for the zoo.

3. My (computer, mother, bedroom) says that I always get (clean, dirty, heavy) when I've been (playing, working, calling) football in the park.

4. Mr Bell has several (goldfish, beehives, caravans) in the (bath, hand, pond) in his (garden, pool, lawn).

5. The little (steps, hills, birds) are hungry in this cold (draught, weather, cupboard) and have difficulty finding (food, directions, paper).

6. (Mr, Mrs, Miss) Turner always (laughed, ate, broke) his breakfast in (his, her, its) kitchen.

Choose the word or phrase that makes each sentence true.

Example A LIBRARY always has (posters, a carpet, <u>books</u>, DVDs, stairs).

> Think about what the word in capitals <u>has</u> to have.

7. A SOFA always has a (pink cushion, seat, stain, patterned cover, cat).

8. A FIRE always has (sticks, big flames, smoke, a fireguard, an oven).

9. A BOILED EGG always has a (chicken, yolk, chip, spoon, nest).

10. A WORD always has (books, people, news, mouths, letters).

11. An OCTAGON always has eight (legs, arms, sites, sides, people).

Underline the one word in brackets that will go equally well with both the pairs of words outside the brackets.

Example rush, attack   cost, fee   (price, hasten, strike, <u>charge</u>, money)

> Look for a word that goes well with both pairs of words. Sometimes the answer from the brackets has two very different meanings.

12 breeze, gale   twist, turn   (curl, gust, wind, roll, current)

13 obvious, clear   simple, ordinary   (easily, bright, front, plain, correct)

14 hike, march   stroll, amble   (stagger, toddle, walk, stride, tread)

15 spin, circle   chance, go   (try, opportunity, twirl, roll, turn)

16 caring, gentle   sort, variety   (kind, charitable, type, class, breed)

17 mark, label   trample, crush   (plod, stamp, trudge, brand, print)

Find and underline the two words that need to change places for each sentence to make sense.

Example She went to <u>letter</u> the <u>write</u>.

18 We were feeling warm so we ran about to cold ourselves up.

19 If you see carefully, you can look three dragonflies over the pond.

20 Mark poured chocolate sauce on the bowl in his pudding.

21 I missed yesterday school as I was feeling unwell.

22 My older brother is learning to car a drive.

23 I dropped by bus ticket my mistake.

Fill in the crosswords so that all the given words are included. You have been given one letter as a clue in each crossword.

> Use the given letter to place definite words.

24   Z

CAMELS
ZIMMER
TREMOR
ENZYME
EXCITE
MELLOW

25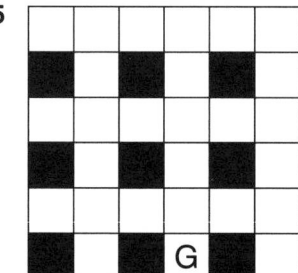

QUIVER
FLINGS
FLASKS
STRESS
LOUDLY
SAVING

26

GRATES
TERROR
REMARK
SKILLS
ORDEAL
TALENT

27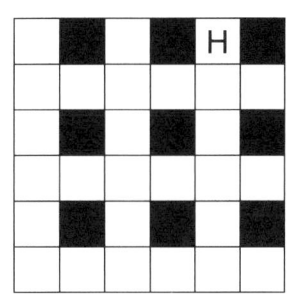

ASLEEP
PARISH
HEARTS
EMPIRE
STREET
PROPER

28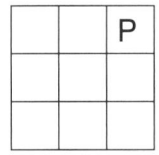

PLY   OIL   HOP
HAS   SLY   AIL

29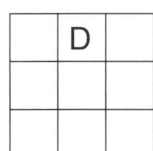

ADD   DRY   ATE
DYE   EYE   TRY

30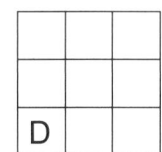

HOD   ORE   IRE
TEN   DEN   HIT

Focus test 5 — Selecting letters

Which one letter can be added to the front of all of these words to make new words?

Example _are _at _rate _all   **c**

1. crumble, crack, clamp, charm — **c**
2. write, wall, waddle, wrapper — **w**
3. valley, vague, van, vice — **v**
4. bridge, beach, barrow, buses — **b**
5. knight, knickers, knot, know — **k**

Find the letter that will end the first word and start the second word.

Example drow (n) ought

6. branc (**h**) otter
7. bull (**y**) outhful
8. fishe (**s**) orry
9. beetl (**e**) ndless

Find two letters that will end the first word and start the second word.

Example pas (ta) ste

10. spri (**ng**) sting
11. climb (**ed**) itor
12. simp (**le**) ttuce
13. bir (**th**) orny

Find the letter that will complete both pairs of words, ending the first word and starting the second. The same letter must be used for both pairs of words.

Example mea (t) able   fi (t) ub

14. shrim (**p**) eople   lum (**p**) atch
15. playin (**g**) ate   sun (**g**) reen
16. spin (**e**) gg   skat (**e**) xercise
17. matte (**r**) ange   wate (**r**) ippling

Move one letter from the first word to the second word to make two new words.

Example   hunt   sip   <u>hut</u>   <u>snip</u>

> Take one letter at a time from the first word and see if you can make a separate word. Then place the letter into the second word until you have made a new word.

18 frail   coal   _____   _____

19 flame   rile   _____   _____

20 proud   moth   _____   _____

21 steal   rains   _____   _____

22 lather   sell   _____   _____

Add one letter to the word in capital letters to make a new word. The meaning of the new word is given in the clue.

Example   PLAN   simple   <u>PLAIN</u>

> Add suitable letters to the word in capitals and think about the meaning to help you. Alternatively, look at the meaning and find a word that uses the letters given on the left.

23 WATER   server   _____

24 TABLE   pill   _____

25 PRICE   a king's son   _____

26 MINER   bodyguard   _____

Remove one letter from the word in capital letters to leave a new word. The meaning of the new word is given in the clue.

Example   AUNT   an insect   <u>ANT</u>

27 BELLOW   under   _____

28 STRAIN   blemish   _____

29 STABLE   musty   _____

30 SCREAM   ointment   _____

Now go to the Progress Chart to record your score!   Total 30

Focus test 6 — Finding words

Find the three-letter word that can be added to the letters in capitals to make a new word. The new word will complete the sentence sensibly. Write the three-letter word.

Example   The cat sprang onto the MO.   USE

1. That dog cleverly caught the B before it bounced.   _____
2. The out-of-control car CRED into a fence.   _____
3. Next year, when I move up a class, Mr Owen will be my CHER.   _____
4. It is so wet that the football CH is flooded at one end.   _____
5. Mrs Khan is my FAVITE teacher at school.   _____

Change one word so that the sentence makes sense. Underline the word you are taking out and write your new word on the line.

Example   I waited in line to buy a <u>book</u> to see the film.   ticket

> Read the sentence carefully to identify the incorrect word.

6. My brother Archie is 12 and she is older than me.   _____
7. The cook carved the joint of lamb with a sharp spoon.   _____
8. Ethan's black eye was so swollen he could not hear very well.   _____
9. Koala bears and kangaroos come from Africa.   _____
10. Grandma likes to sit in her bus next to the fire and by the window.   _____

Change the first word of the third pair in the same way as the other pairs to give a new word.

Example   bind, hind   bare, hare   but, <u>hut</u>

11. quite, quit   plume, plum   stare, _____
12. look, leak   boot, beat   moon, _____
13. mint, lint   mime, lime   mane, _____
14. spoon, soon   flame, fame   grave, _____
15. often, ten   grate, ate   shore, _____

> See how the letters have been changed and continue the pattern. Take care with letter order.

Underline two words, one from each group, that go together to form a new word. The word in the first group always comes first.

Example (hand, <u>green</u>, for)   (light, <u>house</u>, sure)

16 (arm, leg, feet)   (stool, chair, corner)
17 (for, be, by)   (why, cause, stall)
18 (grand, small, big)   (stand, clock, night)
19 (any, those, mine)   (think, one, pile)
20 (dine, eat, sup)   (pose, fling, hurt)

Find a word that can be put in front of each of the following words to make a new, compound word.

Example   cast   fall   ward   pour   <u>down</u>

21 side   shore   spring   hand   _____
22 model   market   man   store   _____
23 pin   cut   dresser   brush   _____
24 dial   glasses light   bathe   _____
25 leader   side   master   worm   _____

Try common prepositions such as up/down, on/in, and colours such as black/white.

Write the four-letter word hidden at the end of one word and the beginning of the next word in the sentence. The order of the letters may not be changed.

Example   We had bat<u>s and</u> balls.   *sand*

Scan quickly to see if you can spot the answer. Check the vowels. Then work through the sentence, word by word.

26 Pigeons can fly very gracefully sometimes.   _____
27 Mrs Mears kindly asked us all to the party.   _____
28 His teacher went through the instructions again.   _____
29 They were all to blame for breaking the china ornament. _____
30 Don't stare at that computer screen all day!   _____

Focus test 7 — Substitution and alphabetical order

If a = 5, b = 2, c = 7, d = 3 and e = 9, find the value of the following calculations.

1. be + (c − a) = _____
2. a^2 − e = _____
3. (d + e) ÷ b = _____
4. 3d + 2a = _____
5. c × (b + d) = _____

Replace the letters with numbers and work out the sums.

Using the same values, find the value of the following calculations. Write each answer as a letter.

6. (a + d) − 3b = _____
7. (a + c) − (e ÷ d) = _____
8. (c + d) − (a − b) = _____
9. de − a^2 = _____
10. 2c − e = _____

If r = 4, e = 7, d = 3, a = 1 and t = 2, what are the totals of these words?

11. tear _____
12. read _____
13. date _____

Add each of the letter values together to make a word total.

GARAGE   HOUSES   BASKET   PASTRY   ENGINE

14. If these words are put into alphabetical order, which comes fourth? _____

COUPLE   CRADLE   CLAMPS   CURLED   CALLED

15. If these words are put into alphabetical order, which comes fifth? _____

BURNLEY   NORWICH   NEWBURY   EXETER   NEWARK

16 If these towns are put into alphabetical order, which comes third? _____

PURPLE   PRICKLE   PRIEST   PRIMLY   PLEASE

17 If these words are put into alphabetical order, which comes first? _____

A B C D E F G H I J K L M N O P Q R S T U V W X Y Z

If the days of the week are put into alphabetical order, which comes:

18 first? _____

19 last? _____

20 the one before Tuesday? _____

21 in the middle? _____

If the letters in the following words are arranged in alphabetical order, which letter comes in the middle?

22 PADLOCK ____

23 BURROWS ____

24 KINDLES ____

Write the letters of the word in alphabetical order, then pick out the middle one.

If the letters in the following words are arranged in alphabetical order, which letter comes in sixth place?

25 FRIZZLE ____

26 SMASHED ____

27 PLASTER ____

Which word in each line contains only the first six letters of the alphabet?

Example	defeat	farce	abide	<u>deaf</u>	dice
28	feeble	fable	faced	famed	foaled
29	bread	bacon	baled	abbot	beaded
30	above	cabbage	cable	faded	beach

Now go to the Progress Chart to record your score! Total 30

Focus test 8 — Word progressions

Look at the first group of three words. The word in the middle has been made from the two other words. Complete the second group of three words in the same way, making a new word in the middle of the group.

Example   PAIN   INTO   TOOK   ALSO   SOON   ONLY

> Look carefully at the first set of three words. Sometimes the pattern is straightforward.

1 PARK   PALE   LENT   FACT   FADE   DELL
2 SOON   HOOK   HULK   BEEN   FEED   FIND
3 BITE   LAMB   LAME   TOOK   SORT   SORE
4 BURN   BUSY   COSY   KISS   KING   LUNG
5 FILM   SILK   SUCK   GATE   PATH   PUSH
6 BOTH   OVER   VERY   STAY   THAN   HAND
7 EVIL   HIVE   GASH   DRIP   BIRD   KERB
8 MOVE   DOVE   DULL   BORN   CORN   CALF
9 WALK   WORN   BORN   PRAY   PORK   FORK
10 GLUE   CLUE   BACK   MILD   WILD   YAWN
11 HARK   HEAT   FRET   NAVE   NEAT   FRET

> In these questions, letters have to be worked out individually as there may be several options with repeated letters.

12 WIRE   WINE   MINE   JOKE   JOIN   VEIN
13 LUSH   BUSH   BATH   DECK   PECK   POOL
14 ARCH   BEAR   BEAN   IDLE   GRID   GREY
15 WASH   WISH   SHIP   LOTS   LETS   CREW

Change the first word into the last word by changing one letter at a time and making a new, different word in the middle.

Example CASE   _CASH_   LASH

> Write down the letters that remain the same. Substitute the remaining letters one at a time.

16 VAIN _____ GAIT
17 PILE _____ PINT
18 CURB _____ HURL
19 JEEP _____ KEEL
20 YAWN _____ YARD
21 PAGE _____ POLE
22 FILL _____ MILK
23 DATE _____ CARE
24 BONE _____ PONY
25 LIVE _____ FIRE

Change the first word into the last word by changing one letter at a time and making two new, different words in the middle.

Example CASE   _CASH_   _WASH_   WISH

> Make sure both the words in the middle are proper words.

26 ZONE _____ _____ TORN
27 FIST _____ _____ DASH
28 JUMP _____ _____ LAME
29 GATE _____ _____ WAVY
30 TILL _____ _____ FIRM

Now go to the Progress Chart to record your score! Total 30

Focus test 9 — Logic

Read the first two statements and then underline the one option that must be true.

> Look for the one statement that <u>must</u> be true, given the information.

1. When the sun rises, it is called dawn. Dawn happens every morning.
   - A It is sunny each morning.
   - B The sun sets in the evening.
   - C The sun rises every morning.
   - D Sometimes it rains.

2. The golden eagle is a bird of prey. Birds of prey are a type of bird.
   - A Eagles are a type of bird.
   - B Birds lay eggs.
   - C Golden eagles live in mountainous areas.
   - D All birds of prey have sharp beaks.

3. Eloise and Hope are twins. They have an older brother, Tom.
   - A Tom was five when the twins were born.
   - B Tom has two younger sisters.
   - C Eloise was born before Hope.
   - D Tom helps to look after the twins.

Four children are wearing different coloured clothes. Amelie and Bart are wearing blue tops. Cameron and Dermot are wearing white tops. Amelie and Dermot are wearing blue jeans. Cameron and Bart are wearing black jeans.

4. Who is wearing a blue top and blue jeans? _____
5. Who is wearing a white top and blue jeans? _____
6. Who is wearing a blue top and black jeans? _____
7. Who is wearing a white top and black jeans? _____

In a test at school out of a total of 20 marks, Maisy got half marks. Tanya got only four answers correct, while Ruby only made nine mistakes. Raj made six mistakes and Dean got three more wrong than Ruby.

> **First, work out the marks each child received.**

8   Who got the most marks? _____

9   Who got the fewest marks? _____

10 Who got fewer than Maisy but more than Tanya? _____

11 Who got four fewer marks than Raj? _____

12 How many did Maisy and Ruby score together? _____

Ben's house is opposite mine. My house is number 24. I live on the even side of the road, he lives on the odd side. There are 44 houses altogether. If number 1 is opposite number 2 and number 3 is opposite number 4 and so on, answer these questions.

13 What number is opposite 11? _____

14 What is Ben's house number? _____

15 One of my next-door neighbours lives at number 22. What number is my other next-door neighbour? _____

16 Kevin lives in a house, on my side of the road, six digits higher than my house number. What number is the house opposite Kevin's? _____

17 The Patel twins live at the far end of the street on Ben's side but a higher number. What number is their house? _____

Samit has £105 more savings than Zao, who has £31 less savings than Reuben. Paul has £21 more than Samit. Reuben has £63. Work out how much each person has.

18 Zao _____

19 Samit _____

20 Paul _____

Six ingredients are in a line on the kitchen shelf. Using the information, give the position of each ingredient on the shelf.

A	B	C WHITE SUGAR	D	E	F

LEFT   RIGHT

The flour is next to the brown sugar which is next to the white sugar. The pasta is at one end of the shelf. The rice is not next to either of the sugars. The rice is to the left of the flour and to the left of, and next door to, the salt.

> Write a list of the ingredients. Eliminate the possible places as you read through the information.

21 The flour ____

22 The brown sugar ____

23 The pasta ____

24 The rice ____

25 The salt ____

Mrs Jones was 25 when she gave birth to her first child. She has two children, two years apart. If her younger child is now 7, work out how old Mrs Jones and her elder child are now.

26 Mrs Jones ____

27 Her elder child ____

If yesterday was Thursday, answer these questions.

28 Which day of the week was it a week ago from today? ____

29 What is the day after tomorrow? ____

30 What day was it four days ago? ____

Now go to the Progress Chart to record your score!   Total

Focus test 10 — Simple codes

In these codes, letters, numbers or symbols may be used to replace letters in words.

If the code for STOCKING is 7 8 3 4 2 0 1 9, encode each of these words using the same code.

First line up the code with the word.

S T O C K I N G
7 8 3 4 2 0 1 9

Then substitute the letters for numbers.

1 SOCK _____   2 COIN _____

Decode these words using the same code.

3 4 3 7 8 _____   4 2 1 3 8 _____

If the code for PRECIOUS is < * ^ % > / \ ~, encode each of these words using the same code.

5 PURE _____   6 ICES _____

Decode these words using the same code.

7 ~ / \ * _____   8 % / * ^ _____

If the code for BIRTHDAY is g n k s z q j p, encode each of these words using the same code.

9 DIRT _____   10 BATH _____

Decode these words using the same code.

11 s k j p _____   12 p j k q _____

Match the right word to each code given below.

FEEL   LEAF   FILE   FAIL
S O H P   S P P H   S R O H   H P R S

> Look for some letters that stand out. Here, all the words begin with F except one, and FEEL also has double E. Once you have solved one, you can work out the others.

13 S P P H _____   14 S R O H _____

15 S O H P _____   16 H P R S _____

17 Using the same code, decode H O S P.   _____

18 If the code for HOLSTER is d g j k m b v, encode SHOT.   _____

19 Using the same code, decode v b k m.   _____

20 If the code for FLAVOUR is ↗ ↓ ↖ ↑ ← → ↙, encode LOAF.   _____

21 Using the same code, decode ↗ ← → ↙.   _____

22 If the code for STICKER is D W Y U P J Z, decode P Y D D.   _____

23 Using the same code, encode REST.   _____

24 If the code for TRACKED is 7 9 3 5 2 6 4, decode 4 6 3 9.   _____

25 Using the same code, encode CART.   _____

If the code for TEACHERS is D 8 # m f 8 5 =, encode each of these words using the same code.

26 CHEAT _____   27 REACH _____

> Make sure you write down the code accurately.

Decode these words using the same code.

28 m f # = 8 _____

29 m 5 8 = D _____

30 # m f 8 = _____

Focus test 11 — More complicated codes

A B C D E F G H I J K L M N O P Q R S T U V W X Y Z

Example If the code for CAB is 3 1 2, work out the codes for these words in the same way.

> Look at the numbers and find the link with the alphabet. In the example, A is the first letter of the alphabet, C is the third, and so on.

1. HIDE _____
2. BEAD _____
3. CAGED _____

Using the same code, what do these codes stand for?

4. 6 1 3 5 4 _____
5. 2 5 1 3 8 _____

A B C D E F G H I J K L M N O P Q R S T U V W X Y Z

Example If the code for CAT is D B U, work out the code for DOG.   E P H

> Look at the relationship between each of the letters and its code. In the example, the code for each letter is the next letter in the alphabet.

6. If the code for BRAVE is C S B W F, work out the code for TIMID. _____
7. If the code for MOUSE is L N T R D, what does S Q T S G stand for? _____
8. If the code for KINGS is J H M F R, work out the code for QUEEN. _____
9. If the code for TAKES is U B L F T, what does N J O V T stand for? _____
10. If the code for FLAME is h n c o g, work out the code for WATCH. _____
11. If the code for NUDGE is m t c f d, what does e h q d r stand for? _____
12. If the code for LUMPS is J S K N Q, work out the code for WINDY. _____

13 If the code for HEDGE is J G F I G, what does I C V G U stand for? _____

14 If the code for SORRY is q m p p w, work out the code for THINK. _____

15 If the code for RAVEN is u d y h q, what does g r y h v stand for? _____

A B C D E F G H I J K L M N O P Q R S T U V W X Y Z

Example If the code for BACK is Z Y A I, work out the code for ZEBRA. <u>X C Z P Y</u>

Think of the alphabet as a continuous line, XYZAB ... and BAZYX ... In the example, two back from B is Z and two back from A is Y, and so on.

16 If the code for WEARS is V D Z Q R, work out the code for CRASH. _____

17 If the code for EVERY is G X G T A, work out the code for AMAZE. _____

18 If the code for GUESS is E S C Q Q, work out the code for CABLE. _____

19 If the code for BLAST is Z J Y Q R, what does Z P C Y I stand for? _____

20 If the code for MAPLE is O C R N G, what does E T C B A stand for? _____

21 If the code for BUDGE is Y R A D B, what does X Y L S B stand for? _____

A B C D E F G H I J K L M N O P Q R S T U V W X Y Z

Example If the code for PEACH is O F Z D G, work out the code for APPLE. <u>Z Q O M D</u>

This time the pattern alternates, letter by letter. If two letters in a word are the same, they are not necessarily the same code letter.

22 If the code for PEACE is Q D B B F, work out the code for CRIME. _____

23 If the code for RISKS is S H T J T, work out the code for SPELL. _____

24 If the code for SPIKE is T O J J F, what does T O F D E stand for? _____

Focus test 1: Words that are similar (pages 4–5)

1. BOG
2. BELT
3. LEAVE
4. FIND
5. CLUE
6. RAISE
7. **roam, wander** 'Roam' and 'wander' mean to travel about or ramble.
8. **harbour, port** Both these are safe places for ships to go to load or unload.
9. **slip, slide** 'Slip' and 'slide' both mean to lose one's footing on slippery ground.
10. **pathetic, pitiable** 'Pathetic' and 'pitiable' both mean wretched or miserable.
11. **neat, tidy** Both words mean well-organised.
12. **lie, recline** Both words mean to be horizontal.
13. **calm, serene**
14. **warm, tepid**
15. **bulk, mass**
16. **wind, meander**
17. **hurry, rush**
18. **swelling, lump**
19. **part** A 'part' can be a share of something and fits in with the other words as they are all part of a whole.
20. **Wednesday** All the words are days of the week.
21. **Thames** All the words are rivers in England.
22. **hazard** 'Hazard' means a danger or menace like the other words.
23. **sister** 'Sister' is a close relation like mother, father, brother. The others are relations but slightly further away.
24. **pant** 'Pant' means to breathe heavily, as do the other words.
25. **murmur** 'Howl' and 'wail' are synonyms meaning to make a loud noise. The synonym of 'whisper' is 'murmur'. Both words mean to speak quietly.
26. **basic** 'Higher' and 'advanced' are synonyms meaning of a very good standard. The synonym of 'lower' is 'basic'. Both words mean of a less than average standard.
27. **positive** 'Bright' and 'shiny' are synonyms meaning polished or shining. The synonyn of 'cheerful' is 'positive'. Both words mean looking on the bright side of life.
28. **silly** 'Ripe' and 'mature' are synonyms meaning ready to eat. The synonym of 'foolish' is 'silly'. Both words mean idiotic.
29. **exterior** 'Internal' and 'inside' are synonyms. The synonym of 'external' is 'exterior'. Both words mean on the outside.
30. **fame** This is a word trick. In the first pair, 'bind' is very similar to 'blind' except the 'l' has been taken out. Similarly, if you remove the 'l' from the word 'flame', you are left with 'fame'.

Focus test 2: Words that are opposite (pages 6–7)

1. SHINY
2. DARK
3. RICH
4. SIMPLE
5. ROUGH
6. SHOUT
7. **hold, release** If you 'hold' something, you clasp it. If you 'release' something, you let it go.
8. **busy, idle** 'Busy' means doing something productively whereas 'idle' means lazy.
9. **open, shut** If a door is 'open', you can pass through it. If it is 'shut', you cannot.
10. **timid, bold** 'Timid' means easily scared whereas 'bold' means confident and brave.
11. **asleep, awake** If you are 'asleep', you are unaware whereas if you are 'awake', you are aware.
12. **slow, quick** 'Slow' means unhurried whereas 'quick' is fast.
13. **high, low**
14. **plus, minus**
15. **grand, humble**
16. **strong, weak**
17. **work, play**
18. **best, worst**
19. **valuable** If something is 'worthless', it has no value or worth whereas something 'valuable' has a high value or worth.
20. **lethargic** 'Lively' means energetic whereas 'lethargic' means lacking in energy.
21. **sink** 'Float' means to be buoyant and stay on the surface of water whereas 'sink' means to fall through the water to the bottom.
22. **foolish** 'Serious' means grave or sensible whereas 'foolish' is silly and thoughtless.
23. **normal** 'Peculiar' is odd whereas 'normal' is ordinary.
24. **tough** 'Tender' means sensitive whereas 'tough' means resilient and hard.
25. **coarse, wet** The other words mean flimsy.
26. **wolf, fox** The other words are members of the cat family.

27 **part, portion** The other words mean complete or all there.
28 **brave, unjust** The other words mean foolish.
29 **mortar, cement** The other words are types of naturally occurring stone.
30 **peace, calm** The other words all mean to stir up.

Focus test 3: Sorting words (pages 8–10)

1–4 Category A Breeds of dog (**terrier**, **boxer**)
Category B Colours (**blue**, **red**, **green**)
Category C Footwear (**sandal**, **boot**, **slipper**, **shoe**)
Category D Body parts (**arm**, **chest**, **head**)
1 B, A, A
2 C, D, C
3 B, C, C
4 D, D, B
5 midday, twelve
6 Sunday, cinema
7 plates, second
8 Spring, season
9 shaved, beard
10 kitten, curtains
11 SPARE
12 SHELF
13 SMILE
14 CHEAP
15 STARE
16 CHEAT
17 LEAST, TALES
18 ANGEL, GLEAN
19 BROTH, THROB
20 THORN, NORTH
21 STONE, NOTES
22 SNARE, NEARS
23 **globe** There is no 'o' in BLEEDING.
24 **stain** There is no 't' in SPRAINED.
25 **gloss** There is only one 's' in APOLOGIES.
26 **marsh** There is no 'r' in SHAMEFUL.
27 proud
28 ashen
29 scant
30 throb

Focus test 4: Selecting words (pages 11–13)

1–6 Try each of the words in the first set of brackets. Do they make sense with any of the words in the second and third sets of brackets? Only one combination of three words makes sense.

1 bought, tickets, Spain
2 train, stops, station
3 mother, dirty, playing
4 goldfish, pond, garden
5 birds, weather, food
6 Mr, ate, his
7 **seat** A 'sofa' is designed to be sat on so it must, above other things, have a 'seat'.
8 **smoke** 'Smoke' is a sign of a 'fire'. It is not 'big flames' as a fire may burn by glowing but it always smokes.
9 **yolk** A 'yolk' is part of an egg.
10 **letters** A 'word' is composed of 'letters'.
11 **sides** An 'octagon' is a two-dimensional figure with eight 'sides'. It does not contain the other elements.
12 **wind** A 'wind' is a current of air, like a breeze or a gale; to 'wind' (with a different pronunciation) means to twist or turn.
13 **plain** If something is made 'plain' it is obvious and clear; 'plain' also means simple or ordinary.
14 **walk** 'Walk' can be used as a noun and verb, and can mean a long trek, like a hike, or a gentle, slow-paced saunter like a stroll.
15 **turn** To 'turn' means to spin or to move in a circle; a 'turn' can also mean an opportunity to have a go at doing something.
16 **kind** To be 'kind' is to be loving and gentle to someone. A 'kind' also means a type of something.
17 **stamp** A 'stamp' is a mark that labels something; to 'stamp' on something means to trample or crush it.
18 We were feeling **cold** so we ran about to **warm** ourselves up.
19 If you **look** carefully, you can **see** three dragonflies over the pond.
20 Mark poured chocolate sauce on the **pudding** in his **bowl**.
21 I missed **school yesterday** as I was feeling unwell.
22 My older brother is learning to **drive** a **car**.
23 I dropped **my** bus ticket **by** mistake.
24

E	N	Z	Y	M	E
X		I		E	
C	A	M	E	L	S
I		M		L	
T	R	E	M	O	R
E		R		W	

25

F	L	A	S	K	S
■	O	■	A	■	T
Q	U	I	V	E	R
■	D	■	I	■	E
F	L	I	N	G	S
■	Y	■	G	■	S

26

■	T	■	T	■	S
R	E	M	A	R	K
■	R	■	L	■	I
O	R	D	E	A	L
■	O	■	N	■	L
G	R	A	T	E	S

27

A	■	P	■	H	■
S	T	R	E	E	T
L	■	O	■	A	■
E	M	P	I	R	E
E	■	E	■	T	■
P	A	R	I	S	H

28

H	O	P
A	I	L
S	L	Y

29

A	D	D
T	R	Y
E	Y	E

30

H	I	T
O	R	E
D	E	N

Focus test 5: Selecting letters
(pages 14–15)

1. **c** crumble, crack, clamp, charm
2. **w** write, wall, waddle, wrapper
3. **v** valley, vague, van, vice
4. **b** bridge, beach, barrow, buses
5. **k** knight, knickers, knot, know
6. **h** branch, hotter
7. **y** bully, youthful
8. **s** fishes, sorry
9. **e** beetle, endless
10. **te** sprite, testing
11. **ed** climbed, editor
12. **le** simple, lettuce
13. **th** birth, thorny
14. **p** shrimp, people; lump, patch
15. **g** playing, gate; sung, green
16. **e** spine, egg; skate, exercise
17. **r** matter, range; water, rippling
18. **r** fail, coral
19. **f** lame, rifle
20. **u** prod, mouth
21. **t** seal, trains
22. **h** later, shell
23. **WA<u>I</u>TER**
24. **TABLE<u>T</u>**
25. **PRI<u>N</u>CE**
26. **MIN<u>D</u>ER**
27. **BELOW**
28. **STAIN**
29. **STALE**
30. **CREAM**

Focus test 6: Finding words
(pages 16–18)

1. **ALL** ball
2. **ASH** crashed
3. **TEA** teacher
4. **PIT** pitch
5. **OUR** favourite
6. <u>she</u>, **he** My brother Archie is 12 and he is older than me.
7. <u>spoon</u>, **knife** The cook carved the joint of lamb with a sharp knife.
8. <u>hear</u>, **see** Ethan's black eye was so swollen he could not see very well.
9. <u>Africa</u>, **Australia** Koala bears and kangaroos come from Australia.
10. <u>bus</u>, **chair** Grandma likes to sit in her chair next to the fire and by the window.
11. **star** The pattern is to remove the last letter (e) from the first word.

12 **mean** The pattern is to remove the second and third letters, 'oo', and replace them with 'ea'.
13 **lane** The pattern is to remove the first letter, 'm', and replace it with 'l'.
14 **gave** The pattern is to remove the second letter.
15 **ore** The pattern is to remove the first two letters.
16 **armchair**
17 **because**
18 **grandstand**
19 **anyone**
20 **suppose**
21 **off** offside, offshore, offspring, offhand
22 **super** supermodel, supermarket, superman, superstore
23 **hair** hairpin, haircut, hairdresser, hairbrush
24 **sun** sundial, sunglasses, sunlight, sunbathe
25 **ring** ringleader, ringside, ringmaster, ringworm
26 **scan** Pigeon**s can** fly very gracefully sometimes.
27 **skin** Mrs Mear**s kin**dly asked us all to the party.
28 **saga** His teacher went through the instruction**s aga**in.
29 **real** They we**re al**l to blame for breaking the china ornament.
30 **area** Don't st**are a**t that computer screen all day!

Focus test 7: Substitution and alphabetical order (pages 18–19)

1 **20** (2 × 9) + (7 − 5) = 18 + 2 = 20
2 **16** (5 × 5) − 9 = 25 − 9 = 16
3 **6** (3 + 9) ÷ 2 = 12 ÷ 2 = 6
4 **19** (3 × 3) + (2 × 5) = 9 + 10 = 19
5 **35** 7 × (2 + 3) = 7 × 5 = 35
6 **b** (5 + 3) − (3 × 2) = 8 − 6 = 2; 2 = b
7 **e** (5 + 7) − (9 ÷ 3) = 12 − 3 = 9; 9 = e
8 **c** (7 + 3) − (5 − 2) = 10 − 3 = 7; 7 = c
9 **b** (3 × 9) − (5 × 5) = 27 − 25 = 2; 2 = b
10 **a** (2 × 7) − 9 = 14 − 9 = 5; 5 = a
11 **14** 2 + 7 + 1 + 4 = 14
12 **15** 4 + 7 + 1 + 3 = 15
13 **13** 3 + 1 + 2 + 7 = 13

14–17 Arrange the words in a grid to make it easier to put them in the correct alphabetical order, then add numbers.

14 **HOUSES**

G	A	R	A	G	E		3
H	O	U	S	E	S		4
B	A	S	K	E	T		1
P	A	S	T	R	Y		5
E	N	G	I	N	E		2

15 **CURLED**

C	O	U	P	L	E		3
C	R	A	D	L	E		4
C	L	A	M	P	S		2
C	U	R	L	E	D		5
C	A	L	L	E	D		1

16 **NEWARK**

B	U	R	N	L	E	Y	1
N	O	R	W	I	C	H	5
N	E	W	B	U	R	Y	4
E	X	E	T	E	R		2
N	E	W	A	R	K		3

17 **PLEASE**

P	U	R	P	L	E		5
P	R	I	C	K	L	E	2
P	R	I	E	S	T		3
P	R	I	M	L	Y		4
P	L	E	A	S	E		1

18–21 Use a grid to help you:

M	O	N	D	A	Y			2
T	U	E	S	D	A	Y		6
W	E	D	N	E	S	D	A	Y	7
T	H	U	R	S	D	A	Y		5
F	R	I	D	A	Y			1
S	A	T	U	R	D	A	Y		3
S	U	N	D	A	Y			4

18 **Friday**
19 **Wednesday**
20 **Thursday**
21 **Sunday**
22 **K** PADLOCK = ACD**K**LOP
23 **R** BURROWS = BOR**R**SUW
24 **K** KINDLES = DEI**K**LNS
25 **Z** FRIZZLE = EFIL**R**ZZ
26 **S** SMASHED = ADEHM**S**S
27 **S** PLASTER = AELPR**S**T
28 **faced**
29 **beaded**
30 **faded**

Focus test 8: Word progressions
(pages 20–21)

1–15 Use grids as shown below to help work out the missing word.

1 **FADE** — PARK / LENT → PALE; FACT / DELL → FALL

2 **FEED** — SOON / HULK → SULK; BEEN / FIND → FEND

3 **SORT** — BITE / LAME → LAMB; TOOK / SORE → SOOT

4 **KING** — BURN / COSY → CORN; KISS / LUNG → KING (KING)

5 **PATH** — FILM / SUCK → SILK; GATE / PUSH → PATH

6 **THAN** — BOTH / VERY → THEY (?); STAY / HAND → THAN

7 **BIRD** — EVIL / GASH → LIVE→ ...; DRIP / KERB → BIRD

8 **CORN** — MOVE / DULL → ; BORN / CALF → CORN

9 **PORK** — WALK / BORN → ; PRAY / FORK → PORK

10 **WILD** — GLUE / BACK → ; MILD / YAWN → WILD

11 **NEAT** — HARK / FRET → ; NAVE / FRET → NEAT

12 **JOIN** — WIRE / MINE → ; JOKE / VEIN → JOIN

13 **PECK** — LUSH / BATH → ; DECK / POOL →

14 GRID

3*	4			1	2	3*	
A	R	C	H	B	E	A	N

3*	4			1	2	3*	
I	D	L	E	G	R	E	Y

15 LETS

1		3*	4*	3*	4*	2
W	A	S	H	S	H	I	P

1		3*	4*	3*	4*	2
L	O	T	S	C	R	E	W

16 **GAIN**
17 **PINE**
18 **CURL**
19 **KEEP**
20 **YARN**
21 **PALE**
22 **MILL**
23 **DARE**
24 **BONY**
25 **FIVE**
26 **TONE, TORE**
27 **FISH, DISH**
28 **LUMP, LAMP**
29 **GAVE, WAVE**
30 **FILL, FILM**

Focus test 9: Logic (pages 22–24)

1 **C The sun rises every morning.** Using the information given, you know that dawn is when the sun rises and it happens every morning. A, B and D may or may not be correct.
2 **A Eagles are a type of bird.** B, C and D are true but A is the only answer that uses the given information.
3 **B Tom has two younger sisters.** As Tom is the twin girls' older brother he must have two younger sisters.
4–7 Use a chart to help you:

	Blue top	White top	Blue jeans	Black jeans
Amelie	✓		✓	
Bart	✓			✓
Cameron		✓		✓
Dermot		✓	✓	

4 **Amelie**
5 **Dermot**
6 **Bart**
7 **Cameron**
8–12 The test is out of 20. Maisy got half marks, therefore 10. Tanya only got 4 right out of 20. Ruby got 9 incorrect, so 20 – 9 = 11. Raj made 6 mistakes, so 20 – 6 = 14. Dean got 3 more wrong than Ruby, so 11 – 3 = 8.
8 **Raj** 14 marks
9 **Tanya** 4 marks
10 **Dean** 8 marks (8 is less than 10 but more than 4)
11 **Maisy** 14 – 4 = 10
12 **21** 10 + 11 = 21
13–17 Use a grid to help you:

1	3	5	7	9	11	13	15	17	19	21	23	25	27	29	31	33	35	37	39	41	43
								-	S	T	R	E	E	T	-						
2	4	6	8	10	12	14	16	18	20	22	24	26	28	30	32	34	36	38	40	42	44

13 **12**
14 **23** My house is 24. Ben's is opposite mine, therefore 23.
15 **26** House 24 is next door to 22 and, on the other side, 26.
16 **29** 6 higher than 24 = 30. Opposite 30 is number 29.
17 **43** Ben lives at 23. The house at the end with a number higher than Ben's is 43.
18 **£32** Reuben has £63. Zao has £31 less than Reuben, so £63 – £31 = £32.
19 **£137** Samit has £105 more than Zao. Q18 tells us Zao has £32, so £32 + £105 = £137.
20 **£158** Paul has £21 more than Samit. Q19 tells us Samit has £137, so £137 + £21 = £158.
21–25 If the brown sugar is next to the white sugar, then it must be B or D, making the flour A or E as it is next to the brown sugar on the other side. As it states the rice is to the left of the flour, the flour must be E rather than A. So the flour = E and the brown sugar = D. As the rice is next to the salt, but not next to either sugar, the rice = A and the salt = B, leaving the pasta at the end of the shelf on F.
21 **E**
22 **D**
23 **F**
24 **A**
25 **B**
26–27 If the younger child is 7, then the older child must be 9 because they are two years apart. If Mrs Jones was 25 when her 9-year-old was born, then 25 + 9 = 34.
26 **34**
27 **9**
28 **Friday** If yesterday was Thursday, today is Friday. A week ago is also a Friday.

29 **Sunday** If yesterday was Thursday, today is Friday, tomorrow is Saturday. Therefore the day after tomorrow has to be Sunday.
30 **Monday** Yesterday was Thursday (1). The day before that Wednesday (2). The day before that Tuesday (3). Therefore four days ago has to be Monday (4).

Focus test 10: Simple codes
(pages 25–26)

1 **7342** S = 7, O = 3, C = 4, K = 2
2 **4301** C = 4, O = 3, I = 0, N = 1
3 **COST** 4 = C, 3 = O, 7 = S, 8 = T
4 **KNOT** 2 = K, 1 = N, 3 = O, 8 = T
5 **< \ * ^** P = <, U = \, R = *, E = ^
6 **> % ^ ~** I = >, C = %, E = ^, S = ~
7 **SOUR** ~ = S, / = O, \ = U, * = R
8 **CORE** % = C, / = O, * = R, ^ = E
9 **q n k s** D = q, I = n, R = k, T = s
10 **g j s z** B = g, A = j, T = s, H = z
11 **TRAY** s = T, k = R, j = A, p = Y
12 **YARD** p = Y, j = A, k = R, q = D
13–17 Three of the words begin with 'F' so LEAF = HPRS. 'FEEL' has a double 'EE' so, therefore, it must be 'SPPH'. Once you know these two words, you can work out the remaining codes.
13 **FEEL** S = F, P = E, P = E, H = L
14 **FAIL** S = F, R = A, O = I, H = L
15 **FILE** S = F, O = I, H = L, P = E
16 **LEAF** H = L, P = E, R = A, S = F
17 **LIFE** H = L, O = I, S = F, P = E
18 **k d g m** S = k, H = d, O = g, T = m
19 **REST** v = R, b = E, k = S, m = T
20 **↓ ← ↖ ↗** ↓ = L, ← = O, ↖ = A, ↗ = F
21 **FOUR** ↗ = F, ← = O, → = U, ╱ = R
22 **KISS** P = K, Y = I, D = S, D = S
23 **ZJDW** R = Z, E = J, S = D, T = W
24 **DEAR** 4 = D, 6 = E, 3 = A, 9 = R
25 **5397** C = 5, A = 3, R = 9, T = 7
26 **m f 8 # D** C = m, H = f, E = 8, A = #, T = D
27 **5 8 # m f** R = 5, E = 8, A = #, C = m, H = f
28 **CHASE** m = C, f = H, # = A, = = S, 8 = E
29 **CREST** m = C, 5 = R, 8 = E, = = S, D = T
30 **ACHES** # = A, m = C, f = H, 8 = E, = = S

Focus test 11: More complicated codes (pages 27–29)

1–5 In these codes, the number corresponds to where the letter is in the alphabet. 'A' is the first letter so equals 1, 'B' is the second so equals 2 and so on.

1 **8945** H = 8, I = 9, D = 4, E = 5
2 **2514** B = 2, E = 5, A = 1, D = 4
3 **31754** C = 3, A = 1, G = 7, E = 5, D = 4
4 **FACED** 6 = F, 1 = A, C = 3, E = 5, D = 4
5 **BEACH** 2 = B, 5 = E, 1 = A, 3 = C, 8 = H
6–15 Compare the code letter with the letter it represents. See how many alphabetical places it has moved and in which direction. Repeat the same pattern in your answers.
6 **UJNJE** To get from the word to the code, move each letter forwards one place.
7 **TRUTH** To get from the code to the word, move each letter forwards one place.
8 **PTDDM** To get from the word to the code, move each letter backwards one place.
9 **MINUS** To get from the code to the word, move each letter backwards one place.
10 **y c v e j** To get from the word to the code, move each letter forwards two places.
11 **FIRES** To get from the code to the word, move each letter forwards one place.
12 **UGLBW** To get from the word to the code, move each letter backwards two places.
13 **GATES** To get from the code to the word, move each letter backwards two places.
14 **r f g l i** To get from the word to the code, move each letter backwards two places.
15 **DOVES** To get from the code to the word, move each letter backwards three places.
16–21 Do these in the same way as 6–15. When you reach the end of an alphabet, wrap round and begin again so XYZ is followed by ABC.
16 **BQZRG** To get from the word to the code, move each letter backwards one place.
17 **COCBG** To get from the word to the code, move each letter forwards two places.
18 **AYZJC** To get from the word to the code, move each letter backwards two places.
19 **BREAK** To get from the code to the word, move each letter forwards two places.
20 **CRAZY** To get from the code to the word, move each letter backwards two places.
21 **ABOVE** To get from the code to the word, move each letter forwards three places.
22–30 Each letter acts separately so check against the code for every letter. Some may go backwards, some forwards.
22 **DQJLF** To get from the word to the code, move the first, third and fifth letters forwards one place. Move the second and fourth letters backwards one place.
23 **TOFKM** To get from the word to the code, move the first, third and fifth letters forwards one place. Move the second and fourth letters backwards one place.

24 **SPEED** To get from the code to the word, move the first, third and fifth letters backwards one place. Move the second and fourth letters forwards one place.
25 **BBMBK** To get from the word to the code, move the first, third and fifth letters backwards one place. Move the second and fourth letters forwards one place.
26 **KNIFE** To get from the code to the word, move the first, third and fifth letters forwards one place. Move the second and fourth letters backwards one place.
27 **g p l f r** To get from the word to the code, move the first, third and fifth letters backwards one place. Move the second and fourth letters forwards one place.
28 **HEART** To get from the code to the word, move the first, third and fifth letters forwards two places. Move the second and fourth letters backwards two places.
29 **f y k q a** To get from the word to the code, move the first, third and fifth letters forwards two places. Move the second and fourth letters backwards two places.
30 **BASIN** To get from the code to the word, move the first, third and fifth letters backwards two places. Move the second and fourth letters forwards one place.

Focus test 12: Sequences
(pages 30–32)

1 **smack, show** 'Slap' is similar to 'smack' in the same way that 'display' is similar to 'show'.
2 **heap, mound** 'Pile' is similar to 'heap' in the same way that 'mound' is similar to 'stack'.
3 **flower, mow** 'Flowers' are 'arranged' in a vase and 'grass' is 'mown'.
4 **Crush, defeat** To 'crush' is similar to 'squash' in the same way that 'overwhelm' is similar to 'defeat'.
5 **sour, fake** 'Sweet' is the opposite of 'sour' in the same way that 'authentic', meaning real, is the opposite of 'fake'.
6 **KL** The sequence is two letters in alphabetical order, one letter missed out, then two more letters in order: AB (C) DE, HI (J) KL.
7 **LK** The sequence is of letters in reverse alphabetical order: RQPO, NMLK.
8 **DW** The sequence starts with the first and last letters of the alphabet, then moves forward from the first letter and backwards from the last letter one place each time.
9 **NZ** Each letter in the first pair moves forwards one place in the second pair.
10 **GV** The first letter in each pair moves forwards one place. The second letter moves backwards one place.
11 **HM** The first letter in each pair moves backwards one place. The second letter moves forwards two places.
12 **QR, UV** After each pair, skip two letters in the alphabet then write the next two: AB (CD) EF (GH) IJ (KL) MN (OP) QR
13 **AC, UW** These are the alternate letters in the alphabet starting with A, arranged in pairs.
14 **UU, WW** This is a repeating pattern moving forwards one alphabetical place.
15 **ZY, VU** These letters are running in reverse alphabetical order.
16 **GZ, KZ** The first letter in each pair moves forwards two places. The second letter is a repeating pattern: YZYZYZ.
17 **RC, OF** The first letter in each pair moves backwards one place. The second letter moves forwards one place.
18 **BR, AU** The first letter moves backwards one place. The second letter moves forwards three places.
19 **WL, QR** The first letter moves backwards two places. The second letter moves forwards two places.
20 **ZA, DE** Each letter in the first pair moves forwards two places in the next pair.
21 **ZY, XW** Each letter in the first pair moves backwards two places in the next pair.
22 **35, 25** Each number decreases by 5.
23 **21, 25** Each number increases by 2.
24 **4, 19** Each number increases by 3.
25 **32, 64** The number doubles each time, so: 2, 4, 8, 16, 32, 64.
26 **11, 16** The number added increases by 1 each time: +1, +2, +3, +4, +5 so: 7 + 4 = 11 and 11 + 5 = 16.
27 **12, 10** The number subtracted decreases by 1 each time: –6, –5, –4, –3, –2 so: 15 – 3 = 12 and 12 – 2 = 10.
28 **4, 6** This is an alternating pattern. The first, third, fifth and seventh numbers increase by 1 each time. The second, fourth, sixth and eighth numbers decrease by 1 each time.
29 **12, 5** This is an alternating pattern. The first, third, fifth and seventh numbers increase by 3 each time. The second, fourth, sixth and eighth numbers decrease by 1 each time.
30 **5, 30** This is an alternating pattern. The first, third, fifth and seventh numbers increase by 10 each time. The second, fourth, sixth and eighth numbers increase by 5 each time.

Mixed paper 1 (pages 33–38)

1. CHOOSE
2. SPEEDY
3. FLAT
4. SHRINK
5. TIRED

6–10 Try each of the words in the first set of brackets. Do they make sense with any of the words in the second and third sets of brackets? Only one combination of three words makes sense.

6. watched, swimming, lake
7. travel, wear, belt
8. triangle, sides, angles
9. lesson, practise, evening
10. cat, fence, garden

11–15 Arrange the words in a grid to make it easier to put them in the correct alphabetical order, then add numbers.

11. **LOCKS**

B	A	R	G	E	1
C	A	N	A	L	3
B	O	A	T	S	2
W	A	T	E	R	5
L	O	C	K	S	4

12. **JUMPS**

J	U	M	P	S	3
J	O	I	N	S	2
K	I	N	G	S	5
J	A	I	L	S	1
K	E	E	P	S	4

13. **FOUNT**

F	A	I	L	S	1
F	I	X	E	S	3
F	O	U	N	T	4
F	E	A	R	S	2
F	U	N	N	Y	5

14. **MEDAL**

M	A	I	N	S	1
M	O	N	E	Y	5
M	I	S	T	Y	4
M	E	D	A	L	2
M	I	N	T	S	3

15. **YEARN**

Y	O	U	T	H		5
Y	E	L	L	O	W	4
Y	A	C	H	T		1
Y	E	A	R	N		3
Y	A	R	D	S		2

16. **CAPE** ❷ = C, ❶ = A, ❺ = P, ❸ = E
17. **PIES** ❺ = P, ❹ = I, ❸ = E, ❻ = S
18. **LEAPS** ❾ = L, ❸ = E, ❶ = A, ❺ = P, ❻ = S
19. ❾❶❷❸ L = ❾, A = ❶, C = ❷, E = ❸
20. ❺❸❶❷❸ P = ❺, E = ❸, A = ❶, C = ❷, E = ❸
21. **k** trick, king
22. **y** worry, yours
23. **h** brush, honest
24. **e** table, each
25. **f** stuff, fudge
26. **happy, merry** 'Happy' and 'merry' both mean cheerful.
27. **beneath, under** 'Beneath' and 'under' both mean below something.
28. **minute, tiny** 'Minute' and 'tiny' both mean very small, miniscule.
29. **bashful, shy** 'Bashful' and 'shy' both mean lacking in confidence.
30. **downy, soft** 'Downy' and 'soft' both mean fluffy and feathery.
31. **U I S P X** To get from the word to the code, move each letter forwards one place.
32. **FRUIT** To get from the code to the word, move each letter forwards three places.
33. **E M G L E** To get from the word to the code, move each letter backwards two places.
34. **FLAPS** To get from the code to the word, move each letter backwards two places.
35. **u b c m f** To get from the word to the code, move each letter forwards one place.
36. **CHARM, MARCH**
37. **VIRAL, RIVAL**
38. **SLEET, STEEL**
39. **STRAW, WARTS**
40. **LEVER, REVEL**
41. **B My dog is black and white.** C may be true, A and D are untrue but B is the only one that uses the information given.
42. **A Alvina had brown bread sandwiches.** B, C and D may be true. A is the only one that has to be true given the information.
43. **Thursday** If yesterday was Wednesday, today is Thursday. Exactly a week from today it was also a Thursday.

44 **Saturday** Today is Thursday, tomorrow is Friday so the day after that will be Saturday.
45 **Monday** Today is Thursday, yesterday (one day ago) was Wednesday, the day before yesterday (two days ago) was Tuesday, the day before that (three days ago) was Monday.
46 **enlarge, increase** 'Shrink' is similar to 'decrease' in the same way that 'enlarge' is similar to 'increase'.
47 **vague, first** 'Certain' is the opposite of 'vague' in the same way that 'final' is the opposite of 'first'.
48 **pick, rush** 'Choose' is similar to 'pick' in the same way that 'hurry' is similar to 'rush'.
49 **bark, moo** 'Dogs' 'bark' in the same way as 'cows' 'moo'.
50 **Woman, boy** A 'woman' is a grown-up 'girl' in the same way as a 'man' is a grown-up 'boy'.
51 **neat** 'Messy' means untidy. The opposite is tidy or 'neat'.
52 **easy** 'Difficult' means complicated. The opposite is simple or 'easy'.
53 **lengthy** 'Brief' means short. The opposite is long or 'lengthy'.
54 **sunny** 'Shady' means out of the sunshine. The opposite is in the light or 'sunny'.
55 **safety** 'Danger' means peril. The opposite is protection or 'safety'.
56 **battery, torch**
57 **computer, games**
58 **inside, behind**
59 **morning, blackbird**
60 **friends, shopping**
61 **off, on** As it's night time and getting dark, the street lights are coming on.
62 **barked, quacked** The duck quacked to warn her ducklings of danger.
63 **jumped, melted** The winter sun shone brightly and the snowman gradually melted away into a puddle.
64 **hair, grass** Toby mowed the lawn as the grass was so long.
65 **three, four** A pack of cards has four suits: hearts, diamonds, spades and clubs.
66 **happy, unsure** The other words all mean unhappy.
67 **violet, indigo** The other words are all shades of red.
68 **increase, class** The other words all mean to grow smaller or weaker.
69 **wind, sun** The other words are all types of precipitation or water from the sky.
70 **heat, bare** The other words all have a double 'oo' in the middle.
71–75 Use grids as shown below to help work out the missing word.

71 **CLAP**

	2		4
S	W	A	N

1		3	
T	I	C	K

	2		4
F	L	I	P

1		3	
C	A	R	T

72 **COOP**

1	2/3*		
G	O	N	E

	2/3*	2/3*	4
M	O	O	D

1	2/3*		
C	A	M	E

	2/3*	2/3*	4
H	O	O	P

73 **TICK**

1	2		
L	E	F	T

		3	4
H	A	N	D

1	2		
T	I	N	Y

		3	4
S	O	C	K

74 **RUSH**

1	2	3	
H	O	L	D

4			
Y	E	A	R

1	2	3	
R	U	S	T

4			
H	O	L	E

75 **CLAY**

1*		3	4
B	O	R	E

1*	2		
B	A	L	M

1*		3	4
B	R	A	Y

1*	2		
C	L	I	P

Mixed paper 2 (pages 39–44)

1

C	O	U	P	L	E
	P		O		L
R	E	F	U	S	E
	N		R		V
S	L	E	E	V	E
	Y		R		N

2

	M		F		T
P	I	L	L	O	W
	N		Y		E
A	C	T	I	O	N
	E		N		T
C	R	A	G	G	Y

3

G		O		B	
L	O	V	E	L	Y
O		E		I	
B	E	R	A	T	E
E		L		H	
S	T	Y	L	E	S

4

A	S	S
S	E	T
H	A	Y

5

E	O	N
G	N	U
G	E	T

6 **24** (6 × 3) + (8 − 2) = 18 + 6 = 24
7 **31** (6 × 6) − 5 = 36 − 5 = 31
8 **2** (2 + 8) ÷ 5 = 10 ÷ 5 = 2
9 **14** (4 × 2) + (2 × 3) = 8 + 6 = 14
10 **16** 2 × (5 + 3) = 2 × 8 = 16
11 **FEW**
12 **LEAVE**
13 **CALM**
14 **SAME**
15 **BEGIN**
16 **HALL**
17 **DAMP**
18 **CORE**
19 **MAST**
20 **FOND**
21 **f** flag, flaw, fox, fright
22 **p** present, preach, party, pitch
23 **w** winter, whose, where, wallow
24 **b** broom, broad, bunion, blast
25 **s** spear, spitting, swearing, snow
26–29 Group 1: musical instruments (**clarinet, trombone**)
Group 2: numbers (**twenty, fifteen**)
Group 3: school subjects (**French, geography, maths, English**)
Group 4: oceans (**Pacific, Indian, Atlantic, Arctic**)
26 **2, 4, 3**
27 **4, 3, 3**
28 **4, 4, 2**
29 **1, 1, 3**
30–31 The children are 3 years apart in age. If the younger one is 14, then the older one would be 17 (14 + 3). Hattie was 22 when her first child was born so she is now 39 (22 + 17).
30 **39**
31 **17**
32–35 Use a chart to help you:

	Big dog	Little dog	Big bone	Little bone	Meaty bone	Gristly bone
Fido	✓		✓		✓	
Brutus	✓		✓			✓
Scruffy		✓		✓	✓	
Ella		✓		✓		✓

32 **Ella**
33 **Fido**
34 **Brutus**
35 **Scruffy**
36 **ke** spike, keyboard
37 **ch** watch, chairman
38 **ll** fill, llama
39 **et** quiet, eternal
40 **er** paler, errand
41 **p 2 9 ∗** K = p, N = 2, I = 9, T = ∗
42 **@ b 3 Y Y** C = @, H = b, E = 3, S = Y, S = Y
43 **NICE** 2 = N, 9 = I, @ = C, 3 = E
44 **SKIN** Y = S, p = K, 9 = I, 2 = N
45 **THINK** ∗ = T, b = H, 9 = I, 2 = N, p = K
46 **water** A 'river' may have other things but it must have water to be a watercourse.
47 **power source** A 'street light' must have power to work so it must have a power source.

48 **claws** 'Claws' are a bear's nails and part of its body.
49 **lead** A 'pencil' needs to have a 'lead' in order to write.
50 **point** A 'needle' must have a sharp end, or point, to go through cloth.
51 **secure, tie**
52 **final, ending**
53 **fight, battle**
54 **fumble, scrabble**
55 **error, mistake**
56 **WIT** witch
57 **BIN** climbing
58 **WAR** swarm
59 **IMP** impressed
60 **OWE** showers
61 **MN** Each letter moves forwards three alphabetical places. Another way to look at this is as an alphabetical sequence with one letter missed out: DF (F) GH; JK (L) MN.
62 **DW** The first letter in each pair moves forwards one place. The second letter moves backwards one place.
63 **EQ** Each letter in the first pair moves forwards one place.
64 **SE** Each letter in the first pair moves backwards two places.
65 **ZA** Each letter in the first pair moves forwards two places.
66 **kill** The pattern is to change the last letter in the first word to 'l'.
67 **ram** The pattern is to remove the first and last letters of the first word, leaving only the middle three letters.
68 **was** The pattern is to remove the last letter.
69 **hare** The pattern is to move the second letter, 'e', to the end of the word.
70 **bide** The pattern is to remove the first letter, 't', and replace it with 'b'.
71–73 If CAB = 312, then A = 1, B = 2, C = 3, D = 4 and so on.
71 **8 9 7 8** H = 8, I = 9, G = 7, H = 8
72 **4 9 3 5 4** D = 4, I = 9, C = 3, E = 5, D = 4
73 **8 5 1 4 5 4** H = 8, E = 5, A = 1, D = 4, E = 5, D = 4
74 **BADGE** 2 = B, 1 = A, 4 = D, 7 = G, 5 = E
75 **BAGGED** 2 = B, 1 = A, 7 = G, 7 = G, 5 = E, 4 = D

Mixed paper 3 (pages 45–50)

1 **distant, near** 'Distant' means far away so the opposite is 'near' meaning close by.
2 **refuse, accept** 'Refuse' means to turn down so the opposite is 'accept' which means to agree to something.
3 **pass, fail** 'Pass' is to do something to an acceptable standard so the opposite is 'fail' which means to do something to an unacceptable standard.
4 **muddle, order** 'Muddle' is confusion or a tangle so the opposite is 'order' which means calm and stability.
5 **pamper, neglect** 'Pamper' means to cosset or look after in a spoiling way so the opposite is 'neglect' which means to ignore or maltreat.
6–10 Arrange the words in a grid to make it easier to put them in the correct alphabetical order, then add numbers.

6 **LUNCH**

L	U	N	C	H		3
B	A	S	I	N		2
A	C	T	I	V	E	1
S	W	E	E	P		5
P	A	N	I	C		4

7 **DUSKY**

D	W	E	L	T	5
D	O	O	R	S	3
D	A	R	T	S	1
D	U	S	K	Y	4
D	I	T	C	H	2

8 **SWEEPS**

S	A	L	T	Y		2
S	W	E	E	P	S	5
S	O	N	I	C		3
S	T	A	B	L	E	4
S	A	F	E	R		1

9 **GLOUCESTER**

G	L	O	U	C	E	S	T	E	R	1
G	R	A	N	T	H	A	M			2
G	R	I	M	S	B	Y				3
H	A	S	T	I	N	G	S			4
W	A	T	F	O	R	D				5

10 **CHEAT**

C	R	A	N	E	5
C	L	O	C	K	3
C	O	A	C	H	4
C	A	T	C	H	1
C	H	E	A	T	2

11 ◊ ● ● ○ □ ◊ = H, ● = E, ● = E, ○ = L, □ = S
12 □ ◊ ● ○ ○ □ = S, ◊ = H, ● = E, ○ = L, ○ = L
13 ◊ △ – ● □ H = ◊, I = △, V = –, E = ●, □ = S
14 **GIVES** △ = G, △ = I, – = V, ● = E, □ = S
15 **SLING** □ = S, ○ = L, △ = I, ∩ = N, △ = G
16 **n** blow, never
17 **r** bathe, wring
18 **r** down, burns
19 **l** fight, clover
20 **e** breath, yearn
21 **HAIL, HALL**
22 **DEED, FEED**
23 **SHOW, SLOW**
24 **BEAT, BEST**
25 **MOAT, MEAT**
26 **Q F O O Z** To get from the word to the code, move each letter forwards one place.
27 **Z O O K D** To get from the word to the code, move each letter backwards one place.
28 **D Z S Q Z** To get from the word to the code, move the first, third and fifth letters forwards one place. Move the second and fourth letters backwards one place.
29 **FAIRY** To get from the code to the word, move the first, third and fifth letters backwards one place. Move the second and fourth letters forwards one place.
30 **PEACH** To get from the code to the word, move the first, third and fifth letters forwards one place. Move the second and fourth letters backwards one place.
31 **childhood**
32 **barrow**
33 **headache**
34 **beeline**
35 **upon**
36 **AB, EF** This is a sequence of letters in alphabetical order, arranged in pairs. After Z, the alphabet starts from the beginning again with A.
37 **CG, GK** Each letter moves forward one place.
38 **ZH, XG** The first letter in each pair moves backwards two places. The second letters are in a repeating pattern: GHGHGH.
39 **AZ, CX** The first letter moves forward by one place each time. The second letter moves backwards one place.
40 **OG, LX** The first letters are in a repeating pattern: OLOLOL. The second letter in each pair moves backwards three alphabetical places.
41 **D**READS
42 **T**HATCH
43 **C**LIMBS
44 STA**B**LE
45 THOUGH**T**
46–50 Lily: 1 or 4 because she cannot be 7 or 8 (she's not sitting next to a friend) or 10 (as Axel is behind her).
Priya: 4 or 10 because she cannot be 7 or 8 (she's not sitting next to a friend) and she cannot be in 1 (she's in an even-numbered seat).
Axel: 4 or 8 because he cannot be 1 (Lily is in front of him) or 7 (he's in an even-numbered seat) or 10 (Jack is behind him).
Jack: 7, 8, 10 because he cannot be 1 or 4 (both Lily and Axel are in front of him).
Sophie: 4, 8, 10 because she cannot be 1 or 7 (she's in an even-numbered seat).
Looking at the possibilities, only Jack can be 7. As Axel and Lily have to be in front of Jack, Axel must be 4 (an even-numbered seat) and Lily 1. So Priya is 10 and Sophie 8.
46 1
47 10
48 4
49 7
50 8
51 **fair** 'Fair' can mean just or honest; it can also describe a nice day without rain.
52 **side** 'Side' can mean the edge or border of something, as well as a team or club of players.
53 **band** 'Band' can mean a group or gang; it can also be a strip or belt (for example, a band of colour).
54 **walk** To 'walk' can mean to stroll or to wander; 'walk' can also be used as a noun – for instance 'a fast walk' can mean the same as 'a fast pace' or 'a fast stride'.
55 **wave** A 'wave' is an effect on the surface of water caused by wind and tide; to 'wave' is to signal or beckon.
56 **winter** All the words are seasons of the year.
57 **peaceful** All the words mean restful or tranquil.
58 **slip** 'Slip' can mean to lose one's footing but here it means a small mistake.
59 **drip** All the words refer to a small amount of liquid dropping.
60 **continue** All the words mean to remain in the same state as before or to persist.
61 **GRIPS**

62 **LAPSE**
63 **BARED**
64 **STRAP**
65 **TRADE**
66 **c** $(3 \times 3) - 7 = 9 - 7 = 2; 2 = c$
67 **d** $(5 \times 4) - (3 \times 5) = 20 - 15 = 5; 5 = d$
68 **c** $(2 \times 3) - 4 = 6 - 4 = 2; 2 = c$
69 **b** $(7 \times 5) - (5 \times 4) = 35 - 20 = 15$. Then $15 \div 5 = 3$; $3 = b$.
70 **a** $(5 + 4) - 2 = 9 - 2 = 7; 7 = a$
71 **9, 5** The numbers decrease by 2 each time.
72 **3, 48** The numbers double each time: 3, 6, 12, 24, 48, 96.
73 **22, 29** The number added increases by 1 each time: +1, +2, +3, +4, +5, +6, +7. 16 + 6 = 22, 22 + 7 = 29.
74 **20, 8** This is an alternating pattern. The first, third, fifth and seventh numbers increase by 5 each time. The second, fourth, sixth and eighth numbers increase by 2 each time.
75 **9, 10** This is an alternating pattern. The first, third, fifth and seventh numbers increase by 2 each time. The second, fourth, sixth and eighth numbers increase by 1 each time.

Mixed paper 4 (pages 51–55)

1 **waste** There is no 'T' in WANDERS.
2 **label** There is only one 'L' in BARNACLE.
3 **shame** There is no 'H' in CLAMBERS.
4 **green** There is only one 'E' in MANAGERS.
5 **forest** There is no 'O' in FIERCEST.
6 The baby was asleep in his **pram** in the **garden**.
7 It is **time** you went to **bed**.
8 I'm **really sorry** but I've broken a glass.
9 Please **come** in and **sit** down.
10 Let's go to the **park** and fly our **kites**.
11 **showy** All the words mean garish, flamboyant or loud.
12 **hasty** 'Swift' means fast and 'slow' is the opposite; in the same way 'steady' means calm or deliberate whereas 'hasty' means rushing.
13 **freezing** 'Warm' and 'cool' are opposites as 'warm' is on the way to be hot whereas 'cool' is on the way to being cold. In the same way, 'boiling' is extremely hot and 'freezing' very cold.
14 **lengthy** 'Brief' is very short and 'prolonged' is very long. In the same way, 'short' is brief and 'lengthy' long-lasting.
15 **cruellest** 'Kindest' is the superlative or extreme end of 'kind' in the same way as 'cruellest' is the most 'cruel' or unkind you can be.
16 mild, strong
17 trivial, important
18 fresh, sweltering
19 lasting, fleeting
20 export, import
21 **M** FAMOUS = AF**M**OSU
22 **U** SUPERB = BEPRS**U**
23 **L** FAMILY = AFI**L**MY
24 **B** ZEBRAS = A**B**ERSZ
25 **S** UNISON = INNO**S**U
26 **11** $5 + 1 + 3 + 2 = 11$
27 **12** $3 + 1 + 6 + 2 = 12$
28 **15** $2 + 4 + 1 + 6 + 2 = 15$
29 **9** $3 + 1 + 1 + 4 = 9$
30 **17** $5 + 6 + 3 + 2 + 1 = 17$
31 **s** guess, swallow; says, silly
32 **d** find, desk; said, distant
33 **w** pillow, went; thaw, whisker
34 **z** jazz, zip; quiz, zone
35 **r** order, risk; milder, root
36–40 Charlotte got six wrong and therefore scored 19. Poppy scored five less than Charlotte, therefore 14. Isaac got two less than Poppy, therefore 12. David scored half Poppy's score, therefore 7. Joshua scored twice David's score, therefore 14.
36 **Charlotte**
37 **14**
38 **7**
39 **14**
40 **5** $12 - 7 = 5$
41–45 All the words begin with 'D' except LAID, so the code for LAID must be F H P O. The code for 'L' is 'F', so DINE must be O P K M as this code does does not include 'F'. From this you know that the code for 'I' in DINE is 'P' so DIAL = O P H F. This leaves DEAL = O M H F.
41 **DINE** O = D, P = I, K = N, M = E
42 **DIAL** O = D, P = I, H = A, F = L.
43 **LAID** F = L, H = A, P = I, O = D
44 **DEAL** O = D, M = E, H = A, F = L
45 **LINE** F = L, P = I, K = N, M = E
46 **OTTER**
47 **SORES**
48 **SCENT**
49 **HEART**
50 **FATHER**
51 **birth** birthday, birthplace, birthmark, birthstone
52 **shoe** shoebox, shoelace, shoemaker, shoestring
53 **door** doorstep, doorbell, doormat, doorstop
54 **wood** woodshed, woodwind, woodwork, woodland
55 **short** shortbread, shorthand, shortlist, shortcake
56 **note** We mended the hutch so my rabbit can**not e**scape.
57 **then** Did you bo**th en**joy the film?

58 **sand** We particularly liked the zebra**s and** the gorillas.
59 **this** He kep**t his** finger on the doorbell for some time.
60 **fall** My worst day o**f all** the school days is Wednesday.

61 **HALF**

		3	4
B	O	L	T

1	2		
M	A	S	K

		3	4
C	A	L	F

1	2		
H	A	N	G

62 **BILL**

	2	3	
P	I	T	Y

1			4
W	A	S	H

	2	3	
K	I	L	N

1			4
B	O	W	L

63 **MESH**

		1*	2*
G	A	I	N

3	4	1*	2*
C	H	I	N

		1*	2*
G	A	M	E

3	4	1*	2*
S	H	O	P

64 **FATE**

	2	3	4*
T	O	U	R

1	4*		
P	R	I	M

	2	3	4*
G	A	T	E

1	4*		
F	A	R	M

65 **LESS**

3	2*	1*	
W	E	S	T

4		1*	2*
N	O	S	E

3	2*	1*	
S	E	L	L

4		1*	2*
S	U	R	F

66 **Lm, Nk** The first letter (capital) moves forward two places each time. The second letters (lower case) are in a repeating pattern: kmkmkm.

67 **WD, XC** The first letter in each pair moves forwards one place. The second letter moves backwards one place.
68 **DK, HW** The first letter in each pair moves forwards one place. The second letter moves forward three places.
69 **ZX, HT** The first letter in each pair moves forward two places. The second letter moves backwards one place.
70 **WI, YK** Each letter moves forwards two places.
71 **R N C A U** To get from the word to the code, move each letter forwards two places.
72 **FEVER** To get from the code to the word, move each letter forwards one place.
73 **MAZES** To get from the code to the word, move each letter backwards one place.
74 **Z H D U B** To get from the word to the code, move each letter forwards three places.
75 **BREAD** To get from the code to the word, move each letter forwards two places.

NOTES

25 If the code for BARGE is A B Q H D, work out the code for CANAL.

26 If the code for CARVE is b b q w d, what does j o h g d stand for?

27 If the code for HOUSE is g p t t d, work out the code for HOMES.

28 If the code for GIRLS is e k p n q, what does f g y t r stand for?

29 If the code for ROSES is t m u c u, work out the code for DAISY.

30 If the code for SINKS is U H P J U, what does D Z U H P stand for?

Focus test 12 — Sequences

Complete the following sentences in the best way by choosing one word from each set of brackets.

Example Tall is to (tree, <u>short</u>, colour) as narrow is to (thin, white, <u>wide</u>).

> Look for the relationship between the pairs of statements. The second pairing must be completed in the same way as the first.

1. Slap is to (slip, clap, smack) as display is to (event, show, dance).
2. Pile is to (clothes, heap, grass) as (mound, hill, mountain) is to stack.
3. Arrange is to (flower, fox, fix) as (tall, jump, mow) is to grass.
4. (Crush, Drink, Keep) is to squash as overwhelm is to (undercut, defeat, miss).
5. Sweet is to (sour, taste, shop) as authentic is to (write, genuine, fake).

Fill in the missing letters. The alphabet has been written out to help you.

A B C D E F G H I J K L M N O P Q R S T U V W X Y Z

Example AB is to CD as PQ is to <u>RS</u>.

> In these sequences, both letters are working together. It may help to put your finger on the alphabet line and count the number of spaces.

6. AB is to DE as HI is to ____.
7. RQ is to PO as NM is to ____.
8. AZ is to BY as CX is to ____.

> In these sequences, the letters are working independently.

9. AL is to BM as MY is to ____.
10. DY is to EX as FW is to ____.
11. KM is to JO as IK is to ____.

Give the two missing groups of letters in the following sequences. The alphabet has been written out for you.

A B C D E F G H I J K L M N O P Q R S T U V W X Y Z

Example CQ   DP   EQ   FP   <u>GQ</u>   <u>HP</u>

In these sequences, the letters are working together.

12 AB   EF   IJ   MN   ___   ___
13 ___ EG   IK   MO   QS   ___
14 TT   ___ VV   ___ XX   YY
15 ___ XW   ___ TS   RQ   PO

In these sequences, the letters are working independently.

16 AY   CZ   EY   ___ IY   ___
17 SB   ___ QD   PE   ___ NG
18 FF   EI   DL   CO   ___ ___
19 ___ UN   SP   ___ OT   MV

Give the two missing groups of letters in the following sequences. The alphabet has been written out for you.

A B C D E F G H I J K L M N O P Q R S T U V W X Y Z

Example RS   TU   VW   XY   <u>ZA</u>   <u>BC</u>

Think of the alphabet as a continuous line – XYZAB and BAZYX, and so on.

20 VW   XY   ___ BC   ___ FG
21 FE   DC   BA   ___ ___ VU

Give the two missing numbers in the following sequences.

Example   2   4   6   8   <u>10</u>   <u>12</u>

> Look for the pattern between the numbers.

22   45   40   ___   30   ___   20

23   17   19   ___   23   ___   27

24   ___   7   10   13   16   ___

> Sometimes the increase/decrease is irregular.

25   2   4   8   16   ___   ___

26   1   2   4   7   ___   ___

27   30   24   19   15   ___   ___

> Check for numbers going up and down. If this is the case, look at alternate numbers.

28   1   9   2   8   3   7   ___   ___

29   3   8   6   7   9   6   ___   ___

30   10   ___   20   10   ___   15   40   20

Mixed paper 1

Find a word that is similar in meaning to the word in capital letters and that rhymes with the second word.

Example   CABLE   tyre   WIRE

1 PICK   glues   _____

2 RAPID   weedy   _____

3 EVEN   plait   _____

4 REDUCE   blink   _____

5 SLEEPY   wired   _____

Complete the following sentences by selecting the most sensible word from each group of words given in the brackets. Underline the words selected.

Example   The (children, boxes, foxes) carried the (houses, books, steps) home from the (greengrocer, library, factory).

6 We (watched, ate, climbed) the ducks (queuing, swimming, walking) on the (bus, bath, lake) for ages.

7 When you (sleep, travel, run) in a car, you must (wear, slide, cut) a seat (belt, cushion, arm).

8 A (triangle, square, circle) has three (sides, chances, colours) and three (arms, angles, angels).

9 Every Saturday I have a piano (key, stool, lesson) and I have to (hurry, draw, practise) every (evening, sometime, year) too.

10 Our neighbour's (grandmother, cat, garden) walked along the (fence, ceiling, wire) and jumped into its own (garden, shadow, lake).

BARGE   CANAL   BOATS   WATER   LOCKS

11 If these words are put into alphabetical order, which comes fourth?   _____

JUMPS   JOINS   KINGS   JAILS   KEEPS

12 If these words are put into alphabetical order, which comes third?   _____

FAILS   FIXES   FOUNT   FEARS   FUNNY

13 If these words are put into alphabetical order, which comes fourth? _____

MAINS   MONEY   MISTY   MEDAL   MINTS

14 If these words are put into alphabetical order, which comes second? _____

YOUTH   YELLOW   YACHT   YEARN   YARDS

15 If these words are put into alphabetical order, which comes third? _____

If the code for SPECIAL is ⑥⑤③②④①⑨, decode each of these words using the same code.

16 ②①⑤③   _____

17 ⑤④③⑥   _____

18 ⑨③①⑤⑥   _____

Encode these words using the same code.

19 LACE   _____

20 PEACE   _____

Find the letter that will end the first word and start the second word.

Example   drow (<u>n</u>) ought

21 tric (__) ing

22 worr (__) ours

23 brus (__) onest

24 tabl (__) ach

25 stuf (__) udge

Underline the two words, one from each group, that are the closest in meaning.

Example (race, shop, <u>start</u>)   (finish, <u>begin</u>, end)

26 (brave, polite, happy)   (merry, unhappy, miserable)
27 (beside, beneath, close)   (over, under, through)
28 (minute, hour, clock)   (time, tiny, hands)
29 (closed, thick, bashful)   (rough, impolite, shy)
30 (downy, hard, sour)   (soft, shiny, dour)

A B C D E F G H I J K L M N O P Q R S T U V W X Y Z

Example If the code for CAT is D B U, work out the code for DOG.   <u>E P H</u>

31 If the code for CATCH is D B U D I, work out the code for THROW.

32 If the code for MELON is K C J M L, what does D P S G R stand for?

33 If the code for STOPS is Q R M N Q, work out the code for GOING.

34 If the code for FLIES is h n k g u, what does h n c r u stand for?

35 If the code for CHAIR is d i b j s, work out the code for TABLE.

Underline the two words that are made from the same letters.

Example TAP   PET   <u>TEA</u>   POT   <u>EAT</u>

36 MARSH   SHAME   CHARM   SMEAR   MARCH
37 VIRAL   ROLES   ROVES   RIVAL   LOVER
38 SLEET   STEEL   LEAST   STOOL   LASTS
39 WHIST   WHERE   STRAW   SWEAR   WARTS
40 SAVES   LEVER   EVERY   SAVER   REVEL

Read the first two statements and then underline the one option that must be true.

41 I have a black and white collie. Collies are a type of dog.

  A Collies are always black and white.

  B My dog is black and white.

  C My dog is very old.

  D Dogs are always collies.

42 Alvina made some sandwiches for lunch. She used a brown sliced loaf.

  A Alvina had brown bread sandwiches.

  B Ready-sliced loaves are handy.

  C Alvina's brother prefers white bread.

  D Alvina always has sandwiches for lunch.

If yesterday was Wednesday, answer these questions.

43 Which day of the week was it a week ago from today? _____

44 What is the day after tomorrow? _____

45 What day was it three days ago? _____

Complete the following sentences in the best way by choosing one word from each set of brackets.

Example Tall is to (tree, <u>short</u>, colour) as narrow is to (thin, white, <u>wide</u>).

46 Shrink is to decrease as (enlarge, big, grand) is to (increase, inside, cease).

47 Certain is to (sure, vague, definite) as final is to (first, next, second).

48 Choose is to (pick, reject, choice) as hurry is to (train, walk, rush).

49 Dog is to (collar, bone, bark) as cow is to (milk, moo, field).

50 (Mother, Woman, Pink) is to girl as man is to (brother, boy, son).

Underline the word in the brackets that is most opposite in meaning to the word in capitals.

Example WIDE (broad vague long <u>narrow</u> motorway)

51 MESSY (untidy clean silly neat fair)

52 DIFFICULT (complicated thorough easy muddled clear)

53 BRIEF (short shirt calm lengthy strong)

54 SHADY (sunny dodgy uncertain kind firm)

55 DANGER (peril stormy safety certain movable)

Rearrange the muddled words in capital letters in the following sentences so that they make sense.

Example There are sixty SNODCES <u>seconds</u> in a UTMINE <u>minute</u>.

56 The TTREYBA _____ in my CHTRO _____ needs replacing.

57 He loves to play RECPMOUT _____ MESGA _____ in his spare time.

58 Come SIDENI _____ quickly and close the door HBENDI _____ you.

59 This ROMGNIN _____ I was woken by a BBILCAKRD _____ singing outside my window.

60 She met some RFIEDNS _____ in town to go SPPHOGNI _____.

Change one word so that the sentence makes sense. Underline the word you are taking out and write your new word on the line.

Example I waited in line to buy a <u>book</u> to see the film. <u>ticket</u>

61 As it's night time and getting dark, the street lights are coming off. _____

62 The duck barked to warn her ducklings of danger. _____

63 The winter sun shone brightly and the snowman gradually jumped away into a puddle. _____

64 Toby mowed the lawn as the hair was so long. _____

65 A pack of cards has three suits: hearts, diamonds, spades and clubs. _____

○ 5

Underline the two words that are the odd ones out in the following group of words.

Example	black	<u>king</u>	purple	green	<u>house</u>
66	sad	upset	happy	miserable	unsure
67	crimson	violet	scarlet	indigo	red
68	increase	dwindle	class	lessen	fade
69	rain	snow	hail	wind	sun
70	foot	heat	hoot	boot	bare

○ 5

Look at the first group of three words. The word in the middle has been made from the two other words. Complete the second group of three words in the same way, making a new word in the middle of the group.

Example	PA<u>IN</u>	INTO	<u>TO</u>OK	ALSO	<u>SOON</u>	ONLY
71	SWAN	TWIN	TICK	FLIP	_____	CART
72	GONE	GOOD	MOOD	CAME	_____	HOOP
73	LEFT	LEND	HAND	TINY	_____	SOCK
74	HOLD	HOLY	YEAR	RUST	_____	HOLE
75	BORE	BARE	BALM	BRAY	_____	CLIP

○ 5

Now go to the Progress Chart to record your score!   Total ○ 75

Mixed paper 2

Fill in the crosswords so that all the given words are included. You have been given one letter as a clue in each crossword.

1    POURER
REFUSE
ELEVEN
SLEEVE
COUPLE
OPENLY

2 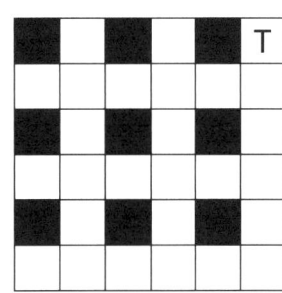   PILLOW
TWENTY
FLYING
MINCER
CRAGGY
ACTION

3 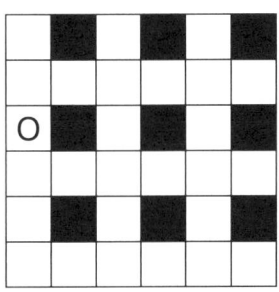   BERATE
LOVELY
STYLES
GLOBES
BLITHE
OVERLY

4 ASS STY
   HAY SET
   SEA ASH

5 EON GNU
   NUT ONE
   EGG GET

If K = 5, M = 6, N = 3, J = 2 and H = 8, find the value of the following calculations.

6 M × N + (H − J) = _____

7 M^2 − K = _____

8 (J + H) ÷ K = _____

9 4J + 2N = _____

10 J × (K + N) = _____

Find a word that is opposite in meaning to the word in capital letters and that rhymes with the second word.

Example SHARP   front   <u>BLUNT</u>

11 MANY   too   _____
12 ARRIVE   weave   _____
13 AGITATED   farm   _____
14 DIFFERENT   claim   _____
15 END   grin   _____

Change the first word into the last word by changing one letter at a time and making a new, different word in the middle.

Example CASE   <u>CASH</u>   LASH

16 HAIL   _____   CALL
17 RAMP   _____   DAME
18 COVE   _____   CORN
19 MUST   _____   FAST
20 FOOD   _____   FIND

Which one letter can be added to the front of all of these words to make new words?

Example __are   __at   __rate   __all   <u>c</u>

21 __lag   __law   __ox   __right   ____
22 __resent __reach   __arty   __itch   ____
23 __inter   __hose   __here   __allow   ____
24 __room   __road   __union   __last   ____
25 __pear   __pitting __wearing __now   ____

Look at these groups of words.

	1	2	3	4
	Musical instruments	Numbers	School subjects	Oceans

Choose the correct group for each of the words below. Write in the number.

26	twenty	___	Pacific	___	French	___
27	Indian	___	geography	___	maths	___
28	Atlantic	___	Arctic	___	fifteen	___
29	clarinet	___	trombone	___	English	___

Hattie was 22 when she gave birth to her first child. She has two children, three years apart. If her younger child is now 14, work out how old Hattie and her elder child are now.

30 Hattie is now ___ years old.

31 Her elder child is now ___ years old.

Four dogs are each chewing on bones. Fido and Brutus are big dogs and have big bones. Scruffy and Ella are little dogs and have little bones. Fido and Scruffy's bones have lots of meat on them. Brutus and Ella's bones are more gristly.

32 Which dog has a gristly small bone? _____

33 Which dog has a meaty large bone? _____

34 Which dog has a gristly large bone? _____

35 Which dog has a meaty small bone? _____

Find two letters that will end the first word and start the second word.

Example   pas (<u>ta</u>) ste

36 spi (__ __) yboard

37 wat (__ __) airman

38 fi (__ __) ama

39 qui (__ __) ernal

40 pal (__ __) rand

If the code for KITCHENS is p 9 * @ b 3 2 Y, encode each of these words using the same code.

41 KNIT   p 2 9 *

42 CHESS   @ b 3 Y Y

Decode these words using the same code.

43 2 9 @ 3   NICE

44 Y p 9 2   SKIN

45 * b 9 2 p THINK

Choose the word or phrase that makes each sentence true.

Example A LIBRARY always has (posters, a carpet, <u>books</u>, DVDs, stairs).

46 A RIVER always has (fish, boats, water, ripples, ducks).

47 A STREET LIGHT always has a (post, power source, parked car, sign, shade).

48 A BEAR always has (a forest, brown fur, a cub, claws, honey).

49 A PENCIL always has a (pencil case, rubber, lead, person, colour).

50 A NEEDLE always has a (point, thread, wool, pin, eyes).

Underline the pair of words most similar in meaning.

Example	come, go	<u>roams, wanders</u>	fear, fare
51	secure, tie	grasp, throw	chase, find
52	start, finish	middle, part	final, ending
53	drip, drop	fight, battle	inspire, expire
54	sun, snow	speed, rash	fumble, scrabble
55	call, beg	error, mistake	fill, fall

Find the three-letter word that can be added to the letters in capitals to make a new word. The new word will complete the sentence sensibly. Write the three-letter word.

Example   The cat sprang onto the MO.   USE

56   Last Hallowe'en I dressed up as a CH.   _____
57   My younger brother wants to play on the CLIMG frame.   _____
58   There is a SM of bees on the branch of that tree!   _____
59   The class RESSED the teacher with their high marks.   _____
60   We fitted in our football game between rain SHRS.   _____

Fill in the missing letters. The alphabet has been written out to help you.

A B C D E F G H I J K L M N O P Q R S T U V W X Y Z

Example   AB is to CD as PQ is to RS.

61   DE is to GH as JK is to _____.
62   AZ is to BY as CX is to _____.
63   AM is to BN as DP is to _____.
64   YK is to WI as UG is to _____.
65   ZA is to BC as XY is to _____.

Change the first word of the third pair in the same way as the other pairs to give a new word.

Example   bind, hind   bare, hare   but, _hut_

66   calf, call   belt, bell   kiln, _____
67   bride, rid   shade, had   frame, _____
68   tiny, tin   seal, sea   wasp, _____
69   wear, ware   bear, bare   hear, _____
70   tall, ball   test, best   tide, _____

A B C D E F G H I J K L M N O P Q R S T U V W X Y Z

Example If the code for CAB is 3 1 2, work out the codes for these words in the same way.

71 HIGH _____

72 DICED _____

73 HEADED _____

Using the same code, what do these codes stand for?

74 2 1 4 7 5 _____

75 2 1 7 7 5 4 _____

Mixed paper 3

Underline the two words, one from each group, that are opposite in meaning.

Example (dawn, <u>early</u>, wake) (<u>late</u>, stop, sunrise)

1. (distant, shiny, bright)   (far, near, remote)
2. (unwanted, refuse, brief)   (accept, rubbish, short)
3. (pass, pick, pull)   (overtake, fail, choose)
4. (instruction, fact, muddle)   (chaos, tangle, order)
5. (pamper, pimple, paddle)   (row, spot, neglect)

    LUNCH   BASIN   ACTIVE   SWEEP   PANIC

6. If these words are put into alphabetical order, which comes third? _____

    DWELT   DOORS   DARTS   DUSKY   DITCH

7. If these words are put into alphabetical order, which comes fourth? _____

    SALTY   SWEEPS   SONIC   STABLE   SAFER

8. If these words are put into alphabetical order, which comes fifth? _____

    GLOUCESTER GRANTHAM GRIMSBY HASTINGS WATFORD

9. If these towns are put into alphabetical order, which comes first? _____

    CRANE   CLOCK   COACH   CATCH   CHEAT

10. If these words are put into alphabetical order, which comes second? _____

If the code for SHELVING is □ ◊ ● ○ − △ ∩ △, encode each of these words using the same code.

11. HEELS _____   12. SHELL _____

13. HIVES _____

Decode these words using the same code.

14. △ △ − ● □ _____   15. □ ○ △ ∩ △ _____

Move one letter from the first word to the second word to make two new words.

Example hunt sip <u>hut</u> <u>snip</u>

16 blown ever _____ _____

17 bather wing _____ _____

18 drown buns _____ _____

19 flight cover _____ _____

20 breathe yarn _____ _____

Change the first word into the last word by changing one letter at a time and making two new, different words in the middle.

Example CASE <u>CASH</u> <u>WASH</u> WISH

21 SAIL _____ _____ HULL

22 DEER _____ _____ FEND

23 SHOD _____ _____ FLOW

24 BOAT _____ _____ VEST

25 MOST _____ _____ MEAL

A B C D E F G H I J K L M N O P Q R S T U V W X Y Z

Example If the code for BACK is Z Y A I, work out the code for ZEBRA.   <u>X C Z P Y</u>

26 If the code for POUND is Q P V O E, work out the code for PENNY. _____

27 If the code for PEARS is O D Z Q R, work out the code for APPLE. _____

28 If the code for TABLE is U Z C K F, work out the code for CARRY. _____

29 If the code for BANGS is C Z O F T, what does G Z J Q Z stand for? _____

30 If the code for MELON is L F K P M, what does O F Z D G stand for? _____

Underline two words, one from each group, that go together to form a new word. The word in the first group always comes first.

Example (hand, <u>green</u>, for)   (light, <u>house</u>, sure)

31 (child, stick, car)   (hat, hood, cap)
32 (low, bar, chair)   (right, pole, row)
33 (sure, might, head)   (ache, string, link)
34 (bee, sting, now)   (hind, line, then)
35 (up, by, one)   (on, there, in)

Give the two missing groups of letters in the following sequences. The alphabet has been written out for you.

A B C D E F G H I J K L M N O P Q R S T U V W X Y Z

Example CQ   DP   EQ   FP   <u>GQ</u>   <u>HP</u>

36 WX   YZ   ___   CD   ___   GH
37 BF   ___   DH   EI   FJ   ___
38 FG   DH   BG   ___   ___   VH
39 ___   BY   ___   DW   EV   FU
40 ___   LD   OA   ___   OU   LR

Add one letter to the word in capital letters to make a new word. The meaning of the new word is given in the clue.

Example PLAN   simple   <u>PLAIN</u>

41 READS   fears   _____
42 HATCH   straw roof   _____
43 LIMBS   mounts   _____
44 STALE   horse shelter   _____
45 THOUGH   believed   _____

Five friends wanted to sit near each other on the bus, but many of the seats were already taken.

From the information, work out where each child sat. The shaded areas on the chart show already occupied seats.

FRONT

1	2
3	4
5	6
7	8
9	10

BACK

Lily and Priya did not sit next to each other or one of their other friends.

Axel sat further forward than Jack but further back from Lily.

Sophie, Axel and Priya sat in even-numbered seats.

46   Lily sat in seat _____.

47   Priya sat in seat _____.

48   Axel sat in seat _____.

49   Jack sat in seat _____.

50   Sophie sat in seat _____.

Underline the one word in brackets that will go equally well with both the pairs of words outside the brackets.

Example   rush, attack   cost, fee   (price, hasten, strike, <u>charge</u>, money)

51   just, honest   fine, sunny   (bright, fair, impartial, clear, cloudless)

52   edge, border   team, club   (squad, fringe, rim, boundary, side)

53   group, gang   strip, belt   (stripe, crowd, crew, band, ring)

54   stroll, wander   pace, stride   (walk, stagger, toddle, wonder, move)

55   breaker, surf   signal, beckon   (flood, ripple, flap, current, wave)

Underline the word in the brackets that goes best with the words given outside the brackets.

Example word, paragraph, sentence (pen, cap, <u>letter</u>, top, stop)

56 spring, summer, autumn (seasons, winter, year, fall, January)

57 unruffled, composed, serene (peaceful, ire, warlike, stormy, weather)

58 error, mistake, blunder (slide, walk, test, trample, slip)

59 trickle, leak, dribble (drip, tap, rain, flood, water)

60 carry on, resume, revive (occur, rest, continue, cease, stop)

Rearrange the letters in capitals to make another word. The new word has something to do with the first two words or phrases.

Example spot	soil	SAINT	<u>STAIN</u>
61 clasps	holds	SPRIG	_____
62 error	failure	SEPAL	_____
63 exposed	uncovered	BREAD	_____
64 belt	leash	PARTS	_____
65 occupation	job	TREAD	_____

If a = 7, b = 3, c = 2, d = 5 and e = 4, find the value of the following calculations. Write each answer as a letter.

66 $b^2 - a =$ _____

67 $de - bd =$ _____

68 $(c \times b) - e =$ _____

69 $\dfrac{(ad - de)}{d} =$ _____

70 $(d + e) - c =$ _____

Give the two missing numbers in the following sequences.

Example 2   4   6   8   <u>10</u>   <u>12</u>

71 13   11   ___   7   ___   3

72 ___   6   12   24   ___   96

73 1   2   4   7   11   16   ___   ___

74 5   2   10   4   15   6   ___   ___

75 3   7   5   8   7   9   ___   ___

Mixed paper 4

Underline the one word in each group that **cannot be made** from the letters of the word in capital letters.

Example	STATIONERY	stone	tyres	ration	<u>nation</u>	noisy
1	WANDERS	waste	draws	swear	wears	wands
2	BARNACLE	crane	learn	cable	label	clear
3	CLAMBERS	lambs	brace	shame	ramble	scare
4	MANAGERS	anger	snare	nears	green	means
5	FIERCEST	fires	fierce	crest	strife	forest

Find and underline the two words that need to change places for each sentence to make sense.

Example   She went to <u>letter</u> the <u>write</u>.

6 The baby was asleep in his garden in the pram.

7 It is bed you went to time.

8 I'm sorry really but I've broken a glass.

9 Please sit in and come down.

10 Let's go to the kites and fly our park.

Look at the pair of words on the left. Underline the one word in the brackets that goes with the word outside the brackets in the same way as the first two words go together.

Example	good, better	bad, (naughty, worst, <u>worse</u>, nasty)
11	gaudy, vulgar	flashy, (showy, explosion, spark, violent)
12	swift, slow	steady, (ready, go, hasty, sluggish)
13	warm, cool	boiling, (tepid, freezing, cold, hot)
14	brief, prolonged	short, (wide, narrow, lengthy, end)
15	kind, kindest	cruel, (dear, expensive, unkind, cruellest)

Underline the pair of words most opposite in meaning.

Example cup, mug   coffee, milk   <u>hot, cold</u>

16 fiery, peppery   mild, strong   spicy, pungent

17 trivial, important   childish, inane   fool, idiot

18 sizzling, scalding   muggy, stuffy   fresh, sweltering

19 endless, long-winded   lasting, fleeting   long, tall

20 baggy, roomy   extensive, varied   export, import

21 If the letters in FAMOUS are arranged in alphabetical order, which letter comes third? ____

22 If the letters in SUPERB are arranged in alphabetical order, which letter comes sixth? ____

23 If the letters in FAMILY are arranged in alphabetical order, which letter comes fourth? ____

24 If the letters in ZEBRAS are arranged in alphabetical order, which letter comes second? ____

25 If the letters in UNISON are arranged in alphabetical order, which letter comes fifth? ____

If r = 4, e = 1, b = 5, s = 3, a = 6 and t = 2, what are the totals of these words?

26 best ____

27 seat ____

28 treat ____

29 seer ____

30 baste ____

Find the letter that will complete both pairs of words, ending the first word and starting the second. The same letter must be used for both pairs of words.

Example mea (<u>t</u>) able   fi (<u>t</u>) ub

31 gues (__) wallow   say (__) illy

32 fin (__) esk   sai (__) istant

33 pillo (_) ent   tha (_) hisker

34 jaz (_) ip   qui (_) one

35 orde (_) isk   milde (_) oot

In a test at school out of a total of 25 marks, Joshua scored more than Isaac and less than Charlotte, who only got six wrong. Poppy scored five less than Charlotte and two more than Isaac. David managed only half Poppy's score. Joshua's score is twice David's.

36 Who scored 19 out of 25? _____

37 Two children scored the same number. What was this number? _____

38 How much did David score out of 25? _____

39 How much did Joshua score? _____

40 How many more did Isaac score than David? _____

Match the right word to each code given below.

| LAID | DIAL | DEAL | DINE |
| O P K M | O P H F | F H P O | O M H F |

41 O P K M _____

42 O P H F _____

43 F H P O _____

44 O M H F _____

45 Using the same code, decode F P K M. _____

Remove one letter from the word in capital letters to leave a new word. The meaning of the new word is given in the clue.

Example AUNT   an insect   <u>ANT</u>

46 POTTER   water mammal   _____

47 SCORES   wounds   _____

48 ASCENT   perfume   _____

49 HEARTH   centre   _____

50 FEATHER   dad   _____

(53)

Find a word that can be put in front of each of the following words to make a new, compound word.

Example cast   fall   ward   pour   <u>down</u>

51 day   place   mark   stone   _____

52 box   lace   maker   string   _____

53 step   bell   mat   stop   _____

54 shed   wind   work   land   _____

55 bread   hand   list   cake   _____

Write the four-letter word hidden at the end of one word and the beginning of the next word in the sentence. The order of the letters may not be changed.

Example We had bat<u>s and</u> balls.   <u>sand</u>

56 We mended the hutch so my rabbit cannot escape.   _____

57 Did you both enjoy the film?   _____

58 We particularly liked the zebras and the gorillas.   _____

59 He kept his finger on the doorbell for some time.   _____

60 My worst day of all the school days is Wednesday.   _____

Look at the first group of three words. The word in the middle has been made from the two other words. Complete the second group of three words in the same way, making a new word in the middle of the group.

Example PA<u>IN</u>   INTO   T<u>OO</u>K   ALSO   <u>SOON</u>   ONLY

61 BOLT   MALT   MASK   CALF   _____   HANG

62 PITY   WITH   WASH   KILN   _____   BOWL

63 GAIN   INCH   CHIN   GAME   _____   SHOP

64 TOUR   POUR   PRIM   GATE   _____   FARM

65 WEST   SEWN   NOSE   SELL   _____   SURF

Give the two missing groups of letters in the following sequences.
The alphabet has been written out for you.

A B C D E F G H I J K L M N O P Q R S T U V W X Y Z

Example CQ DP EQ FP GQ HP

66 Fk Hm Jk ___ ___ Pm
67 UF VE ___ ___ YB ZA
68 CH ___ EN FQ GT ___
69 ___ BW DV FU ___ JS
70 ___ ___ AM CO EQ GS

A B C D E F G H I J K L M N O P Q R S T U V W X Y Z

Example If the code for PEACH is O F Z D G, work out the code for APPLE.   <u>Z Q O M D</u>

71 If the code for QUICK is S W K E M, work out the code for PLAYS.   _____

72 If the code for MUMPS is L T L O R, what does E D U D Q stand for?   _____

73 If the code for FUZZY is G V A A Z, what does N B A F T stand for?   _____

74 If the code for NOUNS is Q R X Q V, work out the code for WEARY.   _____

75 If the code for KNIFE is I L G D C, what does Z P C Y B stand for?   _____